THE ENNEAGRAM FROM A CHRISTIAN PERSPECTIVE

An Enneagram Journey to Self-Discovery and Spiritual Growth

ANDY CONNOR

TABLE OF CONTENTS

INTRODUCTION

There is a wealth of wisdom within us, which is paradoxically a cause of both profound strength and fear. Were it not for our terrible ignorance and unfounded knee-jerk skepticism, we would all learn to pay heed to the world within us and give an answer to the question ever-present in our lives, that is, "Who are you?"

Though faith teaches us that the soul resides within us all and every religion, in some form or the other, pays homage to the soul, what treasures lay locked within, and who dwells in it, these are questions that people rarely concern themselves with. Like most beasts, whether we like it or not, we are forever bound to the materialistic world. But, our psychic sufferings abound when we are not able to find who it is within us that interacts with the world without.

In Christianity, God's grace is understood as the redemption from the false self. But, most people are content with making prayers and supplications to be the beneficiaries of this grace, while paying lip service to a phenomenon that they fail to grasp completely. But, it is a matter of praying as though God was the cause of everything and acting simultaneously as if everything was our doing.

The Enneagram of Personality then arises out of a perspective of human spiritual strivings and seeks to illuminate the depths of the human soul. Undoubtedly then, it is not genuinely Christian but its psychological and non-Christian underpinnings cannot be foregone. That is why the Enneagram adherents occupy various philosophical and religious backgrounds. The Enneagram serves as a bridge where people from different camps are able to come together and have a discussion. Indeed, people from various philosophical and psychological schools have been prime examples of this.

Not only can understanding the Enneagram helps one to identify one's true potential but by doing so one is also able to form a deeper and meaningful relationship with God or the anointed one within. The point where phenomenology, religion, and psychology meet is where the Enneagram and its symbols make itself felt. The Enneagram is not the answer to all your questions but rather a signpost. For it is the 'X' that marks the individual as the bearer of suffering that one is able to, like Christ, cast the light of understanding upon it.

Anyone with eyes can find in one's own face the countenance of God and strive to be more like him. Although each one of us has our demons to cast away and our own ladders to climb to self-actualization, the archetypal patterns of doing so are constant and unchanging.

And, that pattern, which our ancestors figured out long ago, is Christ. Although looking at the Enneagram from the perspective of Christian theology provides a spiritual and religious underpinning, one must never forget that it is also a highly comprehensive cognitive model. A dialectical approach such as this nourishes our understanding of ourselves and gives clarity to how we can build better relationships with the world around us.

I invite you to take a journey through the patterns of the soul and the life within you that has the potential to reach great heights and redeem oneself in the process. Herein, we shall go through the various signs, learn to decode them in a meaningful way, and understand their relevance in our lives today in this modern era.

Just like signposts, the Enneagram only shows us the way, we ourselves have to journey. Though our knowledge may never be complete, it is our duty to realize and do what we can and let the God within us take care of the rest.

Part I: The Enneagram and Christianity

CHAPTER 1

What is the Enneagram?

Enneagram is a portmanteau word made by combining *Ennea* (Greek for 'nine') and *Gramma* (something written or drawn). As such, it is a system of nine personality types that combine traditional wisdom with cognitive psychology to describe how people conceptualize the world and manage their emotions.

As per the Enneagram system, each personality has its own worldview through which it conceptualizes the world that it encounters. This allows one to classify and understand why people act in certain ways. Since the Enneagram is able to describe how personality adapts and responds to challenging and supporting environments, it provides opportunities for personal development while laying down the foundations for understanding others.

There are three major applications of the Enneagram:

- Personal and spiritual growth,

- Developing successful relationships with people,

- And, developing one's ability to work and lead people in the workplace

Since the Enneagram identifies opportunities for growth and self-development, it has been widely used in areas, such as psychotherapy, counseling, parenting, education, business development, etc. Besides, its everyday life application, the Enneagram is also infused with spiritual significance.

In essence, the Enneagram allows us to peek behind the curtain of our consciousness and see which of the coping mechanisms our ego swathes itself in to avoid confronting the pain it has caused us. Until we find the truth about our coping mechanisms, we continue to lie to ourselves and others about who we are.

The nine Enneagram personality types form a wheel, which portrays the basic archetypes of human shortcomings, fears, unconscious desires and needs, etc. It is considered by many people a map that can help one find meaning in one's life and develop a character that can carry one through life, that is, a map that we cannot learn to read until we understand our individual personality or Enneagram type.

CHAPTER 2

Where did the Enneagram originate?

Natural Propensity, Vice to Virtue & Righteous Desire

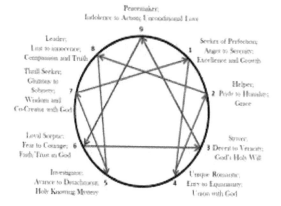

Although the exact origin of the Enneagram system is a contentious issue, a few people believe that its roots can be traced all the way back to the works of Christian mystics in the 4th century. Some scholars go even further and place its origin in classical Greek Philosophy 2,500 years ago or the ancient Babylon period about 4,500 years ago.

The Enneagram has been attributed to Christian mysticism, Jewish Kabbalah, and Sufism. People even consider Dante to have a thorough understanding of the model since many of the characters in The Divine Comedy relate to the nine personality types of the Enneagram.

Ideas similar to the Enneagram are seen in the work of Evagrius Ponticus, who was a Christian mystic. His identification of eight deadly thoughts, a superordinate love for the self, and the remedies to the eight deadly thoughts closely resemble the Enneagram model.

The making of the Enneagram and its figure is associated with G.I. Gurdjieff although he didn't develop the nine personality types that are associated with the model. It is not until Oscar Ichazo started teaching his self-development program in the 1950s that we get our contemporary Enneagram Personality model.

Ichazo's teachings included ideas on ego-fixation, passions, virtues, and holy ideas. He called his teachings 'Protoanalysis' which used the Enneagram figure given by Gurdjieff among many other symbols and ideas. After founding the Arica Institute, he called his method the Enneagram of Personality.

Shortly afterward, the Enneagram of Personality found its way into psychological circles. Thanks to the efforts of eminent psychiatrist Claudio Naranjo and various other psychologists at Berkley, the Enneagram method was incorporated into and combined with modern psychology.

Though the different personality types have been studied in depth separately in the field of psychology, the Enneagram brings them all together under a unified system and highlights their relationship. This unique combination of ancient symbolism with modern psychology continues to fascinate psychologists, educators, and spiritualists alike.

Ever since its implementation in modern Psychology in Berkley, Enneagram – or its modern version at least – has spread through the world at an unfathomable rate. Millions of books have been sold on the subject and various Enneagram programs have sprouted in different countries. Though the method doesn't sell a particular ideology nor does it suggest any set of techniques, it does serve as an effective framework for both religious people and secular practitioners in their lives.

Unlike most psychological frameworks and diagnostic systems that focus solely on the neurotic or damaged side, Enneagram takes into consideration the whole human personality. It describes both the strengths and weaknesses of each personality type. There is no hierarchy and no personality is better or worse. The highs and lows of human nature are found in all nine personality types.

Though most people find the Enneagram of personality to be a system of profound spiritual and personal growth, it has been adapted to other fields of life in recent years as well. For instance, it has been adapted to the educational and business environment to facilitate better human understanding and forging meaningful relationships. Other than providing important "people skills" the Enneagram system also gives focus to good decision making, leadership, self-awareness, and a continual and lifelong learning experience.

Despite its migration to psychological realms, there are certain ideas that remain essential and untouched by the scalpel of modern science. One of the key ideas is that people have two important aspects to them – personality and essence. Every individual has a unique "self" that is his/her essence and cannot be reduced to a category or number.

On the other hand, the Enneagram describes the patterns and themes that constitute a personality, and form one's social persona. In an ideal world, our personality works to effectively express ourselves in the world. However, problems come up when our personality begins to cover up and warp our inner self, and we come in our own way.

The concept of the triad of intelligence has also been wholly incorporated into the modern psychological model of the Enneagram with little or no alterations. According to this, there are three centers of intelligence and perception – Head, Heart, and Body. Each and every one of us has all three of this intelligence, and the different personality types have particular strengths and weaknesses in one of them.

Intellectual Center: Has a penchant for language, rational thinking, ideas, strategies, and plans.

Emotional Center: Characterized by the nature of one's feelings, whether positive or negative, empathy, devotion, and concern for others.

Instinctual Center: Occupies the body for movement, sensory awareness, gut-level understanding, security, and social belonging.

How we view the world and operate depends on the tendencies of our intelligence and perception in these three categories. We must understand where our primary center lies so we are able to develop the potential of our lives and overcome any blind spots that we may have.

CHAPTER 3

How Does the Enneagram System Work?

T here are a few basic things that one will need to know to understand how the Enneagram works. As one will see, there are only a few basic concepts that are required for you to embark on your journey to self-discovery.

The structure of the Enneagram can look a bit intimidating at first though, in reality, it is quite straightforward. There are nine equidistant points on a circle with a number that corresponds to each of them. Number nine, three, and six form an equilateral triangle while the rest of them are connected in this order —one to four, four to two, two to eight, eight to five, five to seven, and seven to one.

One point of view dictates that the nine points correspond to nine predominant personality types. Though something or the other of all personalities can be found in you, there will be one personality type that stands out as being the closest to you.

Most Enneagram authors agree that we have a dominant personality type. This determines, to a large extent, the ways in which we learn and adapt to our early childhood environment. By the time children turn five, they also start to develop a unique sense of self and find ways of fitting into the world.

There are a few things that must be said about the basic personality type:

- People never change from one basic type to another

- The descriptions of the basic personality types are universal. Since no type is masculine or feminine inherently, they apply equally to both males and females.

- At any given time, not all of the basic descriptions will apply since people tend to fluctuate between healthy, average, and unhealthy attributes that make up their personality.

- Numbers are used in Enneagram since they are neutral in terms of value. Furthermore, unlike psychiatric labels, numbers provide an unbiased and shorthand way of describing a number of things about a person.

- No type is better or worse than another. All basic personalities have both assets and liabilities that are unique to them.

The Nine personality types are as follows:

Type 1: The Reformer; seen as being perfectionists, purposeful, and principled.

Type 2: The Helper; seen as being possessive, generous, and demonstrative.

Type 3: The Achiever; seen as being driven, adaptable, and image-conscious.

Type 4: The Individualist; seen as being dramatic, expressive, and self-absorbed.

Type 5: The Investigator; seen as being secretive, innovative, and perceptive.

Type 6: The Loyalist; seen as being responsible, engaging, and anxious.

Type 7: The Enthusiast; seen as being versatile, spontaneous, and scattered.

Type 8: The Challenger; seen as being decisive, willful, and self-confident.

Type 9: The Peacemaker; seen as being reassuring, receptive, and complacent.

The nine personality types are arranged into three Centers. As mentioned before, these three centers are Instinctive Center (Type 8, 9, and 1), Feeling Center (Type 2, 3, and 4), and Thinking Center (Type 5, 6, and 7). The inclusion of a personality center is not done arbitrarily. Instead, each type results from a cluster of characteristics that comprise that Center.

These issues revolve around an unconscious emotional response when there is a loss of contact with one's core self. For the Instinctive center, the predominant emotion is Anger, for Feeling Shame, and Thinking Fear. Needless to say, all personality types contain all emotional responses. However, the basic personality types are especially affected by the Center's emotional theme.

As such, there arises a particular way of coping with the dominant emotional response. Here, we can briefly examine all nine personality types to see what this means.

In the Instinctive center, we have Eights, Nines, and Ones. **Eights** have a knack for acting out their instinctual energies through anger. When an eight feels anger building in them, they respond immediately in a physical way, be either moving forcefully or raising their voices.

Nines tend to deny their anger and are the most out of touch with their instinctive energies. Though they get angry like everyone else, they often feel threatened by their anger.

Ones try to control or suppress their anger and instinctive energies. They believe that they must be able to control their feelings at all times and prefer to direct their energies according to their highly developed inner critic.

Next up, in the Feeling Center, there are Twos, Threes, and Fours. **Twos** try to control their shame by getting other people to like them and think of them as good people. They try to convince themselves that they are of a loving nature by repressing the negative feelings that others stir in them and focusing on the positives.

Threes have a penchant for denying their shame and therefore are the ones that are most out of sync with their feelings of insufficiency. Instead, they manage their shame by trying to be like what they believe a successful person should be like. They can be relentless in their pursuit of success to ward of feelings of shame.

Fours control shame by switching their focus to how special and unique their personal characteristics, talents, and feelings are. They tend to highlight their creativity in order to deal with shame though they are most likely to succumb to those feelings.

Lastly, we have the three personalities in the Thinking Center. **Fives** fear the outside world and believe themselves to be inadequate in their abilities to cope with it. They end up coping by withdrawing from the world. They tend to be secretive, and isolated, and use their minds to learn about the nature of the world. They hope that eventually, through understanding the world on their own terms, they will be able to rejoin but they never feel as though they know enough to enter with total confidence.

Sixes experience their fear as anxiety which severs their connection with their inner knowledge and confidence. They do not trust their own minds and instead look for things outside to make them feel confident. But, no matter how many anchors they create, they are never fully able to clear away the doubt and the anxiety.

Sevens fear their inner world and prefer to steer clear of inner feelings of pain, loss, and anxiety as much as possible. In order to do so, they try to occupy their minds with exciting and stimulating possibilities and distract themselves from their fears. They are mostly seen as chasing one experience after the next and keeping themselves distracted.

The Wing

Every individual is a unique mixture of his/her personality type and one of the two adjacent personalities on the Enneagram circle. These adjacent types are called the wing.

While your basic personality makes up your core, the wing complements and adds important, sometimes contradictory, aspects to your being. Though both wings can have a role to play in one's personality, most people have a dominant wing, meaning one of the two wings is more involved. For purposes of convenience, it is easier to refer to someone's 'wing' as opposed to one's 'dominant wing' as they both mean the same thing.

To fully understand your basic type then, it is important to assess the wing you have. Reading the full description of the two wings and deciding which one applies to you more can help you understand its influence more.

Levels of Development

Within each personality, there is an internal structure which is constituted of one's behaviors, attitudes, motivations, defenses. These make up the nine levels of development in any given personality. Through an understanding of these levels, one is able to see how the various traits are interrelated – how healthy ones can deteriorate into average and unhealthy ones. Understanding these levels also show you how people change within their own personality type.

The nine levels of development are as follows. Bear in mind that two people of the same personality type can seem very different based on which level of development they are at.

Healthy

- Level 1: Liberation
- Level 2: Psychological Capacity
- Level 3: Social Value

Average

- Level 4: Imbalance
- Level 5: Interpersonal Control

- Level 6: Overcompensation

Unhealthy

- Level 7: Violation
- Level 8: Obsession and Compulsion
- Level 9: Pathological Destructiveness

Psychological changes occur at each level. Perhaps the best way to understand these levels is as measures of our capacity to be present. The lower down the ladder we are, the more we identify with our ego and its negativity and restrictive patterns. Our personality becomes more caustic, reactive, defensive, and automatic.

On the other hand, as one moves up the levels, one finds oneself more in the present moment and awake in one's heart, mind, and body. The gradual disappearance of our fixation leads to attunement with the environment. Thus, we are able to see ourselves objectively rather than operating automatically, enslaved to our patterns.

As we become less identified with our personality, we discover that we are able to respond depending on what the environment calls for, bringing forth the potential of the various types, creativity, joy, compassion, strength, and positivity on a whole to whatever we may be doing.

Directions of Growth and Stress

The lines that connect the Enneagram personalities inside the circle denote what each type would do under different conditions. Two lines connect to each type which in turn connects to two other types. The first line connects with a type that shows how the first type would behave when moving in a direction of growth. The other line, connecting to another type, highlights how the person would act when moving in the direction of stress. In simpler terms, different situations will call forth different responses from your core personality.

The Stress direction for each type can be indicated with this sequence, 1-4-2-8-5-7-1. What this signifies is that an average or unhealthy One will behave like an average or unhealthy Four. Similarly, a Four under stress will behave like a Two, and so on. For the rest, the sequence is like this, 9-6-3-9.

On the other hand, the Growth direction is indicated by the reversing the Stress direction.

The sequence then becomes 1-7-5-8-2-4-1 and 9-3-6-9.

Regardless of your personality type, the types that lead to Growth and Stress are important influences on your core type. For a holistic picture then, you can take into your core type, your wing, and the two types in the directions of growth and stress.

The ultimate goal for each personality is to 'move around' and integrate and acquiring the healthy potentials of all nine types. A balanced and fully functional individual is able to draw on the virtues of all types as and when needed. Therefore, it can be said that it is not important which personality type we begin with. Instead, the aim becomes how well we use our type to reach self-actualization.

Another distinction that is important to the understanding of personality is amongst the Three Instincts. This is instinctive intelligence that is necessary for the survival of the individual as well as the species. As such, there is a self-preservation instinct, a sexual instinct, and a social instinct.

Though we all have the three instincts within us, one of them is dominant in our behavior. Then there is the second instinct which supports our dominant instinct, and a third which is the least developed. The organization of these three instincts in our personality creates what is called an "Instinctual Stack".

These instincts or drives profoundly impact our personalities and, at the same time, our personalities determine how we prioritize our instinctive needs, in return. This impact of our personality on our dominant instinct is most prominent when, further down the levels of development, we are caught up in the defenses of our personality.

Each personality type combines with one of the three instincts to yield 27 unique combinations of dominant instincts and types which largely account for the variability and differences within the types themselves. These combinations are termed Instinctual Variants.

CHAPTER 4

The Traditional Enneagram

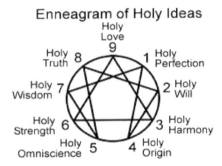

Enneagram of Holy Ideas

Holy Love 9

Holy Truth 8

Holy Perfection 1

Holy Wisdom 7

Holy Will 2

Holy Strength 6

Holy Harmony 3

Holy Omniscience 5

Holy Origin 4

Though the modern-day Enneagram is a synthesis of various ancient traditional wisdom, it wasn't fully formed until Oscar Ichazo brought the seemingly disparate elements of the system together. A brief lesson in history here is due in order to properly understand and appreciate the traditional Enneagram.

Ichazo was born in Bolivia, raised in Peru, and as a young man moved to Buenos Aires in Argentina to learn from a school on inner work. From there, he journeyed through Asia whilst gathering knowledge until his eventual return to South America where he began putting all his knowledge to work and building a system of all that he had learned.

After multiple years of developing his ideas, Ichazo founded the Arica School which functioned as a vehicle for disseminating the knowledge he had received. He taught initially in Chile in the '60s and the '70s before relocating to the United States. While he was still in South America, a group of writers and psychologists went to Arica where they studied with Ichazo and experienced the methods for attaining self-realization which he had developed.

This group of scholars, writers, and psychologists learned the basics of Ichazo's systems and practiced his teachings. The Arica School is a vast system of an intricate and complex body of teachings on metaphysics, spirituality, psychology, cosmology, and so forth which combines the different practices to usher in a transformation of the human consciousness.

Amongst the various teachings was a system of teaching which was based on the ancient symbol of the Enneagram. The symbol finds its roots in the distant past and can be traced back to the works of Pythagoras. As we have already mentioned earlier, the symbol was reintroduced to the world by George Gurdjieff who was the founder of an exceptionally influential school of thought.

George Gurdjieff utilized a series of movements or sacred dance moves to teach the symbol which was designed to provide the participant a felt sense of the meaning of the symbol and its constituent processes. Though Gurdjieff did not teach the types associated with the symbol, he did reveal the chief feature of the types to his advanced students. This was the basic characteristic that defined a person's ego structure.

Gurdjieff used descriptive language to depict a person's chief features, often using Sufi traditions to show people what type of idiot they were. As such, people could be described as square idiots, round idiots, squirming idiots, subjective hopeless idiots, and so on. However, he never taught his disciples about a system concerning the characteristics in relation to the Enneagram symbol.

For such reasons, various early Enneagram aficionados mistakenly attributed the Enneagram system to Gurdjieff and the Sufi because of his utilization of Sufi techniques. Many have succumbed to the widespread, though erroneous, belief that the Enneagram system has its roots in the Sufi or other ancient schools of oral tradition.

Though there is some truth to the claim that Ichazo incorporated the knowledge of these traditions in his understanding, the connection of such esoteric knowledge to the Enneagram symbol was done by him alone. This is why the 'Traditional Enneagram' system reaches only as far back as the 1960s. However, it is well worth noting that the ideas behind the Enneagram system are also found in various mystical traditions such as Islam, Judaism, Christianity, Buddhism, and even Greek philosophy.

The system of the Enneagram that Ichazo taught Americans was slightly different from the one that became widely popularized in the subsequent decades in America. It was based on four primary Enneagrams, or Enneagons as he referred to them. These include the Enneagram of the Passions, Virtues, Fixations, and Holy Ideas.

In order to truly understand these and their internal relationships, we must take into account the fact that this system was built to understand the relationship between the personality (or the Ego) and its essence.

According to Ichazo, the Enneagram is a means of examining the specifics regarding the structure of the human soul. Particularly, it examines how the qualities of the soul Essence end up becoming distorted or compressed into ego states.

Ichazo himself mentions that one must distinguish between a man's ego or personality and his essence. A man is fearless, perfect, and in unity with the whole cosmos in his essence; no conflict can arise within the person or between the person and others. However, as the ego develops and one accumulates karma, a person slowly transitions from objectivity to subjectivity. In other words, he falls from his true essence to his ego or personality.

There is a recurrent theme in Western philosophical traditions – the idea of nine divine forms – which Ichazo drew upon while developing his theories of the Enneagram. The same idea was also discussed as *Divine Forms* by Plato; forms and qualities of existence that are complete in their essence and cannot be broken down further into constituent elements. The same idea was further developed in the 3rd century A.D. by Plotinus in his work *The Enneads*.

From Greece and Asia Minor, these ideas found their way to Egypt where after they were embraced by Christian mystics who started focusing on the study of the loss of Divine Forms in man's ego consciousness. The ways in which these forms end up becoming distorted were soon referred to as the Seven Deadly Sins – avarice, pride, anger, envy, gluttony, sloth, and lust. However, what remains a mystery is how exactly, over the course of a century, the nine forms were reduced to seven deadly sins.

The teachings of mystical Judaism, especially those from the Kabbala have also had an important impact on the development of ideas by Ichazos. The diagram of the Tree of Life is central to the Kabbala. It is referred to as the map that shows the patterns and the laws according to which God has created the universe. This diagram consists of 10 spheres which are linked in particular ways by 22 paths.

It is possible that Ichazo was aware of the Kabbalistic teachings, especially the one that considers all human souls as 'sparks' which emanate from the spheres of the Kabbalistic Tree. According to the Kabbala teachings, every Biblical patriarch is said to embody one of the spheres of the Tree. Such teachings suggest that the different kinds of souls are aspects of the Divine Unity.

Ichazo's brilliance is reflected in his discovering of how all these Divine forms correspond to the Enneagram symbols as well as with the different human intelligence centers, namely, Thinking, Feeling, and Instinctive. Ichazo called the essential quality of the human mind, the higher aspects, Holy Ideas. This is in accordance with the traditional western mystical teachings.

The Holy Ideas also correspond to Holy Virtues. These virtues, when they are abiding in Essence, are considered to be the essential qualities of the heart as they are experienced by humans. Once a person loses presence and self-awareness and falls away from the Essence and into the trance of one's personality, the loss of awareness of the Holy Idea leads to one's Ego-fixation. Furthermore, the loss of contact with Virtue leads to one's Passion.

Though every human being has the capabilities to embody all of the Holy Virtues and Ideas, a single pair of them is central to one's soul's identity. Thus, its loss is felt acutely and the ego becomes preoccupied with recreating it continually and in a self-

defeating way since it is a futile effort, to
begin with.

Virtues, Passions, Holy Ideas, and Ego-Fixations

The Passions and Ego-fixations of a human
being symbolize the various ways in which the
spiritual qualities of one's soul are contracted
into ego states. According to Ichazo and his
teachings, there are a total of nine primary
ways in which one loses one's center and ends
up distorting one's thoughts, feelings, and
actions. Thus, there are a total of nine ways in
which one forgets or severs one's connection
with the Divine. One way to see the Passions
is to consider them as our untamed animal
nature before they are transformed into higher
states through higher-level awareness.

At the same time, one is able to learn to
reconnect with the Divine essence. Since
there is an intimate relationship between the
higher qualities of one's soul and their
equivalent ego distortions, one can, through
presence, awareness, and recognition
recognize the pattern of one's distortion.
These distortions are the characteristics of
passions and ego-fixations.

Thus, one is able to recognize the Essence that has become distorted and obscured over time. By contemplations and remembrance of the higher human qualities, one is able to accelerate one's awareness of one's own Essence, thereby restoring balance. When one knows one's type, one are able to direct one's inner mind to facilitate the process of transformation.

Every being holds within oneself the expansive and non-dual qualities of Essence, which can be experienced through a direct and effective manner when a person is abiding by one's true nature. This is what is described by Virtues. Virtues are, quintessentially, the natural expression of the heart that has awakened. No one has to try to force oneself to become virtuous. Instead, as one relaxes and becomes more present and aware, seeing through and beyond the desires and fears of the ego, such qualities manifest naturally within the human soul.

In an interview, Oscar Ichazo tells that individuals are always within contact with their virtues by simply being alive and living in one's body. It is the subjective mind, the ego, which loses touch with the virtues. The result is that the personality begins to compensate for its loss by developing passions.

One of the underlying emotional responses created as a result of the loss of contact with one's essential nature, with one's true being, one's identity as spirit and essence is represented by the Passions. The grief, the shame, the underlying hurt that such a loss entails is enormous. There is no way but for our ego to become compelled to react in its characteristic ways to cope with the loss. Though the Passion is effective temporally, it is, in the long run, a misguided coping strategy by our ego. However, since the Passion is inherently a distorted version of our essential Virtue, we are able to, in principle, recognize it and restore the Virtue.

In another way, one can also see the Virtue of each type in the Enneagram as an antidote to the Passions, and as the center point for the positive traits of one's type. Passion can be transformed with ease by simply recalling and recognizing the Virtue and being aware of it. If one is to use the Enneagram traditionally and spiritually, it is extremely important that one restores one's Virtue and transform one's Passion effectively.

Lastly, there are Holy Ideas. These can be represented as non-dual perspectives of the Essence – specific ways of understanding and recognizing the unity of being itself. When one is present and awake, these ideas arise naturally in a quiet, clear mind, seeing reality for what it really is. When one loses one's Holy Idea, it again leads to the particular ego delusion that we have mentioned thus far, called Ego-fixation.

Here too, through ego-fixation, the individual is constantly making n effort to reinstate the freedom and balance of the Holy Idea. However, here the ego does it from its dualistic perspective which is yet again a futile endeavor. The only antidote to such an ego-fixation is recognizing and understanding the perspective that is tied to the functioning of one's type's Holy Idea. Only thusly does the non-dual perspective of our true being is completely restored.

This is, in brief, the traditional sense of the Enneagram and its working. As one can see, its origins and history have had a tortuous path. However, its understanding is embedded in traditions and arcane knowledge of the mystics from generations past, which have been preserved in ancient texts and scriptures. The Enneagram then becomes a guide to recovering one's connection with one's true self, and, as such, is a truly spiritual method.

CHAPTER 5

Jesus and the Enneagram

KEY CHARACTERISTICS

THE PEACEMAKER
9

THE CHALLENGER 8   1 THE REFORMER

THE ENTHUSIAST 7   2 THE HELPER

THE LOYALIST 6   3 THE ACHIEVER

THE INVESTIGATOR 5   4 THE INDIVIDUALIST

C hristian spirituality entails a
transformation of the self that can
come about only when both the self
and God are known deeply. As such, there is
no deep understanding of God without
having an understanding of the self, and vice-
versa. If we leave the self out of Christian
spirituality, the transformation is not
grounded in reality or experience and is

therefore not connected to the vicissitudes of life.

Knowing God and knowing the self are two sides of the same coin. This 'double knowledge' is identified as the core tenet of Christian faith and spirituality. In the 18th century, during the age of enlightenment, there was a powerful cultural shift towards intellectualism, rationalism, and reason that ran parallel to skepticism regarding religious orthodoxy. At that time, under the influence of the cultural mood, the Church slowly shifted its focus from experiential knowledge to doctrinal accuracy. As such, self-awareness and self-knowledge was left behind. True understanding has always been relational, above and beyond mere rationalism, doctrinal orthodoxy, and towards experiential.

According to Christian faith, God took on the form of man in the person of Jesus of Nazareth. His visible presence in the material world helped humanity conquer the experiential disconnection and brokenness. What separates Christianity from other religions is its Triune God which took on the form of a man.

Jesus is the character and face of God, the archetypal messiah, the pattern and mode of being that reveals relationships between fellow men and that between man and the divine ought to look like. Since Jesus was both human *and* divine, he is the primary teacher and guide in the pursuit of the double knowledge. His path leads towards reconciliation as well as restructuring the distorted image of God and the self.

In our modern world, people like to assume that they know themselves and that they are fully in control of their thoughts and desires. Rarely do they question how or why they see the world in the way that they do, whether or not our perceptive lens are distorted. Their worldview and its impact on their lives are taken in their strides. Without any sense of awareness, our lives putrefy and lead to disease and brokenness. The single most important practice in spiritual concerns then becomes awareness and presence.

The absence of self-awareness breeds and perpetuates the state of disconnection, ignorance, and hubris. Only through experiential knowledge of God and oneself can embark on one's spiritual journey of waking up. For this reason, the gospel is seen as a vision and promise that leads to transformation. It is the one source that can truly lead to a transformation of one's habits and relationships. It not only heals the heart, mind and the body, but also frees oneself from feelings of shame, anger, and fear.

Our lives are beset with chaos every step of the way and our behaviors, emotions, and thought patterns are subject to an infinite number of modes of living that can lead to destruction. When left on their own devices, things fall apart – for that is the law of entropy, a universal law. The only way to lead one's self out is by embracing the mode of being displayed by Jesus. It is the source of abundant life, purpose, and meaning.

There are many amongst us who are intuitively aware of the pattern of behavior or mode of being that reconnects us with God. However, not everyone is gifted as such. That is why tools such as the Enneagram come in handy. Just like the gospel, it too is a guide for the lost, the broken, and the wicked. A whole man wouldn't need it. But one must be wary of deeming oneself whole when one is torn asunder by one's ego and its worldview.

Various spiritual guides, psychologists, and theologians have thought of the Enneagram as a mirror. It highlights the nine ways one can get lost and nine ways in which one can return to one's true self. The Enneagram, then, can assist one in developing self-awareness, learning to recognize and let go of the things in our lives that are limiting, and welcomes one to look deeper into the mysteries of one's own true identity.

Our attitudes and motivations, which are type-specific according to the Enneagram, uncover and disclose our spiritual blind spots. These spiritual blind spots do not simply result in stumbling about and bruising our souls. These blind spots keep us from knowing and receiving the love of God. As our blind spots are uncovered, motivations exposed, and fears are defenses denuded, a reconciliatory and restorative path is revealed. This clears the path for self-awareness and experiential knowledge of oneself.

The path that was elucidated by Jesus is discovered within every Enneagram type. Since God took the form of man, and that form was Jesus who came to save us all, each of us has the capacity to discover in him our own way of reaching our true potential. Taken together, all the nine Enneagram types are the perfect and unsullied expression of God. As such, we can conclude that Jesus' personality contains within it all nine types.

Scripture tells us that Jesus is the image of God and in him dwells the fullness of God. It is through Jesus that we find out the nature of God. Therefore, both the true self in the form of Jesus and the nature of God can be found within the Enneagram.

A skewed and dysfunctional image of God ends up degrading what it means to be human. The experiential understanding of both the self and God can be revealed in the divine, yet completely human, a person of Jesus. The beauty of the Enneagram system invites us to experience the love of God and reveals the path to deeper self-communion and awareness. Our distorted image of God can recover, which opens the way to transformation. Only when the Enneagram is used as a means to self-discovery does Jesus become a guide into restorative healing.

If we do not take into account the spiritual transformation that can be brought on by the system, all the wisdom of the Enneagram simply ends up becoming a futile intellectual exercise. Perhaps the most supreme action that is undertaken by human beings to welcome the divine into our lives is prayer. The spiritual understanding of the Enneagram allows us to become aware of ourselves as well as others and opens up ever more to the spaces within us where the prayer of the soul is able to thrive. The wisdom that is integral to the Enneagram allows us to inhabit the holy space from where we are able to experience intimacy with God.

The Enneagram describes not only our personality traits but also our inherent motivations. Therefore, it can aid us in emancipating ourselves from the incomplete and mistaken perceptions that we may have regarding ourselves, other people in our lives, and God. Each type can immensely gain by opening up the prayer spaces within itself in order to develop deeper self-awareness and intimacy with the archetypal being that is Jesus.

In this day and age, we are in dire need of spiritual practices that can deliver us from our sufferings, whether or not we want to believe in it. We ignore our inner world and understanding of the divine at our own peril. The Enneagram provides us that structure through, which we can free ourselves from our ego fixations and close identification with our thoughts and feelings.

It can take years of practice to become spiritually empty, to have communion with our inner God, and the nature of God without. If we are full of ourselves, there is no space for anything else, certainly not God. Just as Jesus was tempted in various ways to sever his connection with God, so we find ourselves limited by our capacities to govern ourselves.

There are various instances mentioned in the gospel wherein Jesus shows himself, in his humility, to be the model for true inner knowledge and awareness. Just as our struggles plague our selves, so did his sufferings plague him. However, instead of moving in the direction of Stress or Disintegration, he shows us how to guide ourselves in the direction of Growth and Integration.

Whenever you find yourselves at the crossroads, confused and lost, remember that God created human beings in his image. That means that the divine resides within you, and with self-awareness and presence, you will have clarity of mind. The Enneagram, if not anything else, is the tool that allows one to recognize one's pitfalls and blind spots. As one becomes more and more aware, these can be minimized and worked upon.

There is created, within each person, the unique potential to express God's creative and infinitely loving nature. The humanity of Jesus reveals to us what humans are capable of and what their relationship with themselves and God appears to be. Only through him as our guiding light can we restore our sundered connection with God and reconcile our true identity.

CHAPTER 6

The purpose of the Enneagram

The mind of human beings is wired for survival. As children, we instinctively place a mask, we know as personality, over our authentic selves to protect us from difficulties and inch our way into the world. Made of a lot of other things like defense mechanisms, conditioned reflexes, coping strategies, and innate qualities, our personality helps us sense and know what all we need to please our parents, relate well to our friends, fulfill the expectations of the culture, meet the basic requirements of life, etc.

Over the span of time, adaptive strategies become increasingly complex. They might get triggered in a predictable manner. In fact, it might be done so often and automatically that it becomes very difficult to know when they have ended and when the true nature takes over.

The worst case is when you override who you are with your personality. This is when you lose touch with your authentic self or forget who you really are; this is the very essence that makes up your personality.

The important reason why you should understand your Enneagram 'number' or 'type' is not to replace your personality with another one. Even if it were possible, it would certainly not be the best idea. You actually need an individual personality or you will be left behind in the world.

The overall purpose of your Enneagram is self-understanding and developing beyond the limits and dimensions of your personality. Additionally, you will also improve your relationships and grow love and compassion for the people around you.

According to the Enneagram charts, there are a total of nine different styles of personalities around the world. Each one of us gravitates towards a certain Enneagram type when we are born; we do this to feel safe and cope.

Each number or type has a distinct way of viewing the world and a fundamental motivation will influence how that Enneagram type will behave, feel, and think. Of course, most people tend to object to the idea that there are only nine basic types of personalities in a planet that consists of more than seven billion people.

So, let us take an example. Your spouse is looking for that 'perfect red color' for the bathroom walls and you take her to the nearest Home Depot. Once here, you will find infinite shades of red that can either brighten up your bathroom or could end up wrecking your marriage.

Similarly, while humans can adopt only one of these Enneagram types as a child, you will find an almost limitless number of expressions of each Enneagram type. While some might appear similar to yours, others would be the stark opposite of your type.

However, we can still consider all of them as variants of the same primary color. Learning this powerful knowledge about Enneagram types will change all aspects of your life by developing your EQ or Emotional Intelligence. In turn, it will improve your relationship with your family, friends, and colleagues and increase your self-awareness.

Develops emotional intelligence

You would be surprised to know that the EQ (Emotional Intelligence) accounts for almost 80% of your life's success, while your IQ consists only of 20%. Your emotional intelligence is a combination of interpersonal (social skills and empathy) and intrapersonal (motivation, self-regulation, and self-awareness) intelligence. While IQ is required to solve job or life problems, EQ plays a much important role since it helps us work with other people more effectively, adapt to our environment, and evaluate and regulate our emotions.

Enneagram offers a long-lasting and great solution that will help you in further developing your EQ. EQ affects all components of emotional intelligence, namely social skills, empathy, motivation, self-regulation, and self-awareness. Additionally, you will able to identify the feeling, thinking, behaving, and underlying motivations in yourself and others with great accuracy.

Increases self-awareness

As mentioned above, we take up certain coping strategies very early in life to get along with others and get the essentials of life like self-worth, love, and security. This coping strategy will prove to be beneficial and will serve us well, especially when we are that young. However, these coping strategies tend to remain with us as we grow, and soon become rigid and fixed patterns that cannot be changed; this happens because you get comfortable and familiar with them.

With the help of Enneagram, you will understand what box you are in (even without knowing it) and your repetitive patterns that direct your behaviors, emotion, and beliefs. You will be provided with a map that will guide you to experience and build your strengths and free you from compulsive habits.

Once you understand the type of Enneagram your personality belongs in, you become more aware and mindful of your unconscious motivations and patterns underneath your behavior. You start observing your

imaginations, emotions, feelings, and thoughts
without repressing or judging them. With
regular practice, you become less defensive
and reactive and more conscious of the
choices that you make, thereby becoming
more capable of coming up with a wider
range of coping strategies in your normal
routine.

Improves relationships

Once you are able to change the way you can
relate to your behavior, you can instantly be
able to relate with others easily. Without the
knowledge of Enneagram, you will obviously
believe that every person thinks in the same
way and they have similar priorities, values,
and motivations as we do.

Once you have the Enneagram insight, you
will look at people with a different set of
filters and know that each person has
different priorities, values, and motivations.
This knowledge will help you become more
sensitive towards the difference, experience
their emotions, and see things from their
perspectives. Once you are able to understand
why people do what they do, you become
much less reactive and more empathetic.

With this, real connection and communication become possible because you are not defending yourself, and you become more compassionate to the struggles and sufferings of others. With compassion, your relationships will take a huge stride towards mutual happiness and satisfaction.

CHAPTER 7

Why is the Enneagram so popular among Christians?

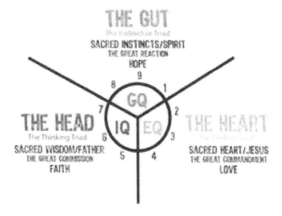

THE CENTERS

THE GUT
The instinctive Triad
SACRED INSTINCTS/SPIRIT
THE GREAT REACTION
HOPE

THE HEAD
The Thinking Triad
SACRED WISDOM/FATHER
THE GREAT COMMISSION
FAITH

THE HEART
SACRED HEART/JESUS
THE GREAT COMMANDMENT
LOVE

W e can say that Enneagram is fairly new to evangelicalism, but it is increasingly gaining popularity and can be found in some evangelical universities. You understand this critique of Enneagram, you need to understand two different and equally important religious worldviews.

The first is the view of Christian theism throughout the ages. According to this theism, it states that the Triune God of the Bible existed as God from all eternity. God as Holy Spirit, Son, and Father existed before anything else was created. This goes on to explain that God is non-contingent and was flawless in all His heavenly attributes before the conception of other things.

Once God created, He is and was transcendent to the creation. The Creator cannot be dependent on His own creation. In Christian theology, this quality is known as 'aseity.'

In today's time, a view is growing popular that denies God's transcendence in important ways; this point of view is also known as panentheism. In the simplest term, panentheism is a term that means 'God's presence is everywhere'. Although Enneagram experts and authors do not claim a certain view, their teachings incorporate philosophies of the East, like Buddhism, and indicate panentheism.

In today's panentheism, the idea that history is linear – starting out of nothing and ending in eternal judgment – is rejected. Additionally, God, being in everything, helps provide credence to the idea of spiritual and social evolution, which is popular with religious ecumenists like Enneagram authors.

According to Christian theism, it states that history is all heading towards judgment. It also states that the fall of the entire human race is affirmed and will be plunged into darkness and sin. All the descendants of Eve and Adam are born spiritually alienated, lost, or dead to God. The plan of God of Messianic salvation is the only way to be saved from eternal judgment.

The Enneagram

The point of Enneagram is to discover the 'true self' and, therefore, find God. It is a circle with nine numbered points at equal distance from each other. Each one of these points is connected with the lines to create three triangles inside the circle. These structures are considered important for understanding the entire Enneagram spiritual scheme.

The nine numbers represent nine personality types. Each of these personalities has its own share of strengths and weaknesses. The processes of spiritual formation taught by the Enneagram are geared towards the person's Enneagram type and have been designed to bring the people back to their child, before the development of any vices.

While Enneagram might seem confusing, Enneagram authors provide numbers on each of the type that explains to you the description of each type. The nine-point geometric figure is loved by Christians for its ability to help a person understand their tendency toward certain sin struggle and disposition.

According to historians, Naranjo was a psychiatrist from Chile and bought the Enneagram back to the US. He later introduced the concept to his students. One of them, Father Robert Ochs, later taught the same to his seminary students at Loyola University. Hence, the Enneagram made its first impressions upon the American Christian circles and only started growing.

Why do Christians love the enneagram?

While 'what's your number' might be a popular pickup line today, it wasn't at the 'Why Christian' event's pre-conference portion. This took place when the event came back at Chicago's Fourth Presbyterian Church for the second time.

This inquiry was just a standard part of the ancient personality typing system that exploded in popularity among different Christian circles. According to Ian Morgan Cron, who led the Enneagram Conference alongside Suzanne Stabile on September 29th, referred to it as 'disruptive spiritual technology.'

However, the truth here is that it is not as modern as it may sound, or alien to religion as others might fear.

Enneagram is not a new system. Some parts of it like the symbol and the nine points within a circle has existed since ancient times. However, the system has launched in the past few years, especially among faith communities who are using it in individual spiritual practice, on retreats, in therapy sessions, and Bible studies.

The roots of Enneagram can be traced to Evagrius, a Christian ascetic and monk who lived in 4th century BC; according to Stabile and Cron, his teachings later influenced the formation of the infamous seven deadly sins. On the other hand, others detected the influence of Enneagram within Judaism and Sufism.

In its current form, Enneagram includes nine different types of numbers or types. Each type, at its worst, is connected to one of the deadly sins – now, two more traits have been added into the mix. Your 'type' can only be determined by self-examination; here, the aim is to better understand your tendencies, strengths, and weakness, along those of others.

Both Stabile and Cron, a type Two and type Four respectively, encountered the book called The Enneagram: A Christian Perspective, which was penned down by the founder of the Center for Action and Contemplation and Franciscan priest of the New Mexico Province, Richard Rohr.

Cron was attending a conservatory seminary at the time and stated that the Enneagram was a 'genius'. The Episcopal priest, songwriter, counselor, and author could not identify anything that conflicted with the gospel.

On the other hand, Stabile contacted Rohr almost immediately after reading the book and started studying under him. Under Rohr, Stabile attended and led more than 500 workshops based on Enneagram for the next 25 years.

The modern system of Enneagram can be traced back to Oscar Ichazo, a Bolivian philosopher during the 1960s; later, his teachings were passed on to Claudio Naranjo, a psychiatrist, who bought it to the United States. Later, Richard Rohr published his studies and findings in the book known as 'The Enneagram: A Christian Perspective', as said above.

When the Enneagram arrived in the US around the 1970s, it initially caught on among Catholic priests and seminarians and became a useful tool for spiritual formation. However, it did not burst into the scene right away. It started taking a gradual descent in the 1970s as an oral tradition only; it was passed down from teacher to student.

Additionally, the teachings were never recorded because some teachers were afraid that if it was written down, the Enneagram would be commercialized and trivialized. However, the books started appearing in the 1980s and then only accelerated forward. Of course, the proof of this fact is the availability of books on how Enneagram can help your spiritual growth, parenting style, sex life, or business.

Of course, some trivialization also took place, but so has a deep spiritual transformation. Today, one of the biggest Enneagram trends is that it is finally being recognized and adopted by traditional religious practitioners, particularly Christians.

The conference chair for International Enneagram Association, Jan Shegda, states that the work of Richard Rohr has been profoundly influential in mapping the intersection and connection of Enneagram and Christian faith. According to Shegda, Rohr was one of the earliest teachers because his spiritual mentor was among the first group to study about Enneagram. Shegda also added that it has created quite a following in the Christian tradition.

The popularity of Rohr opened the possibility for other books of Enneagram and religion, apart from 'The Road Back to You, like Christopher Heuertz's and Stabile's 'The Sacred Enneagram' and 'The Path between Us' respectively, which were published within two years from each other.

According to Jan Shegda, these books are written in a more comfortable language for evangelical readers. The audience feels more understanding and comfortable about what Enneagram is all about.

The religious focus was apparent at the global conference of the International Enneagram Association in 2018, where hundreds and thousands of Enneagram enthusiasts and teachers gathered at Cincinnati.

Several different types of sessions about Enneagram and Christianity were held; additionally, there were also other workshops like the Buddhist approach to the Enneagram. Shegda implied that the two faiths had a formal workshop. In any of the sessions that the audience attended, there were spiritual components in both.

That particular conference also saw a new 'track' for programming that was related to spiritual and personal development.

However, the question remained – why was there a sudden interest in the Enneagram among Christians? Apart from the books from Christian presses, there were now church groups that discussed the Enneagram in several different Protestant congregations like the Presbyterian, Baptist, Methodist, and Episcopal churches that have joined hands with the Roman Catholic parishes in organizing and holding workshops and retreats on the Enneagram.

Cron mentions that his podcast listeners and readers are not interested to be a part of the church. However, they are still interested in spiritual growth. Enneagram is the perfect answer for them since it promises self-knowledge without having to belong to a religion. Cron explains that with the world right now, there are a lot of institutions that can help such people understand the past is gone and will not have much influence on the present.

Centers of intelligence can play a vital role in creating a worship service

Enneagram involves nine different types of personalities. For instance, type one is often known as the perfectionist or the reformer. Two are depicted as the people-pleaser or helper. Three is called the achiever, four is the individualist, and so on.

However, you should not allow stereotypes to define the person. When you are leading with your Enneagram type, it is not the entire story behind you. This is because Enneagram is not a cage; instead, it provides us with a set of keys so that we know that we are dealing with and where we need to focus our attention.

All types of Enneagram are divided according to the intelligence, based on whether they are centered on the gut, head, or heart. These are the factors that play an important role in crafting worship services.

Type twos, threes, and fours mostly lead with their hearts; hence feeling and tone are important factors. It is important for those types to be with others without a role or words. Hence, worship services need to include a separate time of communal silence.

For types five, six, and seven, these people are mostly led by the brain. This is the journey outwards, which means symbols, iconography, and candles are very helpful.

For type one, eight, and nine, they are led by their gut feeling. This is where stories will prove to be useful and give them a sense of worth.

Overall, a good circle of worship needs to include facilities for all the three above-mentioned groups.

Things to consider for Christians while using Enneagram

Some things that you need to remember while using Enneagram are:

The Enneagram helps you with self-reflection; not self-control or sufficiency

As discussed above, Enneagram is a tool that can help you find your path to self-knowledge. With the help of the Enneagram test, all your strengths and weaknesses will be revealed. This will give you the chance to be thankful for your talents and abilities. Enneagram is almost a false promise if you are unable to balance your traits appropriately and find out how to be the best and healthy version of your type.

Your personality matters a lot

Your Enneagram type does not define the person that you are. There is a value in understanding yourself. However, that particular knowledge should not confine you to certain patterns, categories, and even repeated behaviors. Also, filtering people according to the nine Enneagram types will underestimate the creations of God.

Don't allow your personality to become a roadblock to your life's journey

Most Enneagram and personality tests simply point towards the direction where we are special and strong. However, when you are weak, most people will ask you to 'find a balance.' However, feeling weak is just a sign that God wants you to recognize our need for Him. This is something that cannot be manipulated.

CHAPTER 8

Unique Benefits of the Enneagram for Christians

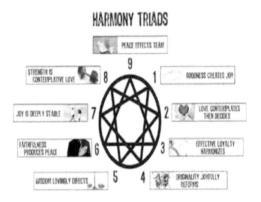

HARMONY TRIADS

PEACE EFFECTS TEAM

9

STRENGTH IS CONTEMPLATIVE LOVE · 8

1 · GOODNESS CREATES JOY

JOY IS DEEPLY STABLE · 7

2 · LOVE CONTEMPLATES THEN DECIDES

FAITHFULNESS PRODUCES PEACE · 6

3 · EFFECTIVE LOYALTY HARMONIZES

WISDOM LOVINGLY DIRECTS · 5

4 · ORIGINALITY JOYFULLY REFORMS

I t is quite ironic and surprising that the Enneagram has gained popularity so quickly, while there are some evangelicals remain suspicious of the tool. Of course, it might probably because it can robustly affirm all your sins. Chuck DeGroat, the Western Seminary professor, recently reminded conservative and skeptical Christians that the

Enneagram has people of all stripes talk about assailing sin patterns.

Just some time back, a certain Evangelical leader condemned Enneagram and mentioned it as an approach that is often at odds with the contours and language of Scripture. However, the Denver Seminary's professor of Christian formation, Howard Baker said that some evangelicals are critical, skeptical, or wary of Enneagram due to an author's interpretation of it; this can be compared to discarding the Bible after reading one liberal comment on it.

While the Enneagram might look like a personality typology for self-knowledge on the surface, it can be used as a tool for stepping into the transformation that God extends to the human race in Christ. However, this tool will be of no use if we are not able to know its purpose in context with the Gospel.

In the simplest terms, Enneagram makes sanctification specific by providing you a roadmap that will take you where you need most of the healing. As asserted by Baker, the nine types that you see in an Enneagram diagram are distinct pathways to transformation.

So, how do you approach the Enneagram as a tool to draw you into the power of the Scripture? You need to engage communally, deeply, and slowly to be truly transformational. While you can choose to take an online assessment, which is the easy way out, the real fruit of Enneagram can only be seen through curious and patient consideration of your life's overall journey.

Here are some unique benefits of Enneagram for Christians:

Appreciating the presence of God

A lot of Enneagram teachers will focus primarily on spirituality; however, they will not talk about your relationship with God. This is something that even some Christian speakers won't do. There are some conferences and talks that make use of examples from the Gospels to show how Jesus embodies each Enneagram type in its perfection. The first and foremost reason to learn about your personality is to grow your love for Jesus and learn how to better serve Him with your life.

Awareness of the soul

We all love to talk and gossip about personality characteristics and preferences at social gatherings. You can also do that with Enneagram, but it is just scratching the surface.

According to Enneagram theory, human personality has been malformed by defense mechanisms, stress, pain, and sin. We have been stripped away from the ever-loving presence of God. We often come up with self-help solutions and it does not work. Most of the time, we do not know what we are doing and end up getting stuck in destructive habits.

By relying on God via the ancient wisdom of Enneagram, you will grow and put on a positive path. For each type of Enneagram, there are levels of what are good and what are bad.

Learning about basic emotional posture

Each type of Enneagram will deny its basic emotional issues with anxiety, shame, or anger. When you're fully self-aware of your feelings and thoughts, you will often choose not to get in touch with your core emotions or underlying sadness over the losses you have suffered.

If you are able to convert your feelings into words, you will receive empathy; this will improve your productivity and relationships. Understanding Enneagram will also help you invigorate your experience of God's wisdom and loving presence.

Godly sorrow for your sin pattern

As mentioned above, the origins of Enneagram can be traced back to Evagrius, a Christian monk in the 4th century; he was the one who identified the deadly sins that we often read about today in human nature. The Enneagram system unravels these nine root sins and transforms them into nine different types of personalities.

We need God's power, grace, and forgiveness through the faith in Christ to cope and heal from our destructive patterns and be transformed according to the image of Jesus.

Calming down your reaction to stress

Once you have an idea about which Enneagram type you fall under, you will be able to predict how you will reach to certain situations. When we face these situations, we subconsciously incorporate the weakness of other types. Once you become aware of this fact, you will be able to make better choices to that you stay attuned to the ever-loving presence of God.

Acknowledging and appreciating your growth opportunity

If you learn about Enneagram types, you will be able to see a path for growth; this is done by identifying the other type's 'face of Christ' that you need to learn from. This way, you will be able to incorporate the strengths of Enneagram and rely on the grace of God to be your own best self.

Feeling empathy for other people

You have to be extremely careful with the typing of personality, especially with the powers of Enneagram. It is not considered nice to use this knowledge to judge people or tell them what Enneagram type they belong to. It is always encouraged that you discover your type by donning on a few types and then find the one that best fits your personality.

If used in the Christ-like way, you will be able to offer grace and empathy to other Enneagram types.

Part II: The Nine Enneagram Personality Types

CHAPTER 9

Enneagram Type 1: The Reformer

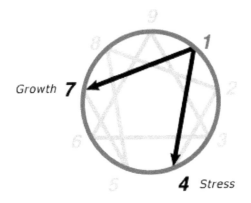

E nneagram Type 1 is called the
reformer. These people are rational,
idealistic, ethical, purposeful,
perfectionists, and self-controlled. Ones are
principled and conscientious while being
aware of what is right and what is wrong.
These people are advocates, crusaders, and
teachers for change.

Type one people always strive higher and try
to improve things but they fear making errors
along the way. They aim to be consistent with

their principles and justify themselves so no one criticizes or condemns them. Ones are fastidious, organized, and disciplined while maintaining high standards.

However, ones can also be perfectionists and critical, generally having anxiety and resentment issues. They are righteous, rational, sharp, intelligent, and morally heroic at their best. The basic desires of ones include being fair, balanced, and good while having integrity. Their basic fears are to become bad, flawed, evil, imbalanced, corrupt, or make mistakes.

Ones are known for their hardworking, responsible, truthful, trustworthy, self-controlled, and realistic nature. They have strong principles. However, like every other personality type, ones too have their weaknesses. They are excessively critical, non-adaptable, angry, judgmental, self-denying, emotionally repressed, and inflexible.

Overview

Healthy Ones

Type one personality is known as the reformer because such people are idealistic and take great efforts to make the world better. They believe that to be worthy, they must do the right and good things. Moreover, their inner critic constantly monitors their actions.

Such people are good superheroes, law enforcers, teachers, judges, or preachers. Type one people are responsible, perfectionists, and obsessed with improvements. Such people essentially try to improve things since they believe that nothing is ever good enough.

This is why people belonging to this type of personality are termed as perfectionists and idealists who wish to reform and bring everything in order. Ones are responsible, loyal, and capable friends and partners. Owing to their firm beliefs, they generally are great leaders who motivate their followers with their concept of excellence.

Generally, reform movements are led by ones. They are honest, dependable, and coherent. This personality type is generally ambitious and driven. Such people are workaholics, active, industrious, dependable, obedient, honest, and practical. They are organized and make lists, which they finish completely. Such people get things done and arrive in the office first and leave at last.

Ones have a lot of talents and interests, which is why they never run out of things to do and are self-reliant. They are rarely impulsive. Moreover, ones are independent and intelligent and can often confuse themselves as Fives. However, unlike Fives, ones take action and not just think about it.

Average Ones

Ones are fastidious. They always know about the defects in themselves, other people, and the various situations they face. This is why they always feel the need to get better, which is good for all the concerned people but is quite taxing for both this personality type as well as the receivers of the reform efforts made by ones.

People with this personality type are serious, rigid, and competent with high principles. They themselves follow the rules as well as want others to follow them and take life seriously like them. Such people are critical of themselves and others.

Ones put a strong emphasis on self-control and personal integrity. They focus on correcting the wrong things and doing the right things. Such people have high standards and distinguish things between white and black, wrong and right. They work hard to always do the right things.

Unhealthy Ones

When ones cannot achieve their desired perfection, they become guilty of failure, which gives rise to anger towards an imperfect world. They also feel guilty about this feeling of anger since they know that anger is not a good feeling, which is why they genuinely and sincerely take efforts to become good.

Due to this, ones strongly repress their anger, which results in occasional fits of rage but more often manifests anxiety, frustration, judgmental criticality, and annoyance. This is why ones are hard to live with. Furthermore, the relentless attitude of one's towards pursuing an ideal lifestyle makes them anxious and leads to depression.

Ones are never able to relax and deny themselves a lot of harmless pleasures of life. And, since ones repress their emotions, they are not able to express their tender feelings to anyone. They view emotions as a sign of a lack of control and weakness. Owing to their anxious nature, they may feel that they are a six. However, unlike sixes, ones don't have to seek affirmation from a group for their standards.

Development Levels

Healthy Development Levels

Level 1

Ones are extremely wise and sharp at their best. They are realistic by accepting the reality and aware of the best action they can take in every moment. Ones are known for being hopeful, inspiring, and kind.

Level 2

Ones are conscientious and have strong personal beliefs. They are well aware of right and wrong and moral values. Moreover, ones aim to be logical, self-disciplined, balanced, mature, and moderate in everything.

Level 3

Ones have strong principles with a strong sense of responsibility and personal integrity. They always try to be ethical, objective, and reasonable. Their primary values are justice and truth. They seek a higher purpose due to which they are generally teachers.

Average Development Levels

Level 4

Ones become discontented with reality and believe that the burden of improving everything is their responsibility. They become high-minded idealists, crusaders, critics, and advocates. Ones go into causes and explain others the way they should be.

Level 5

Ones fear they will make mistakes. They have this constant feeling to follow their ideals consistently and be well-organized and orderly. Moreover, ones become impersonal and puritanical. They severely curb their impulses, emotions, and feelings. Such people are often workaholics, punctual, pedantic, anal-retentive, and fussy.

Level 6

Ones become very critical and judgmental of themselves as well as others. They form opinions about everything and constantly pester and correct other people to do the right things as per their views. Such people are fastidious, perfectionists, impatient, and dissatisfied until the thing is done as per their directions. They are also indignantly angry, rude, scolding, and moralistic.

Unhealthy Development Levels

Level 7

Ones start believing that only they know the absolute truth and everything else is incorrect. Such people become extremely strict in their judgments and rationalize their own actions. They become highly dogmatic, intolerant, self-righteous, and rigid.

Level 8

Ones cannot tolerate the misconduct of others and become obsessive about the flaws of others even though they may engage in contradictory actions and do the opposite of the things they advocate.

Level 9

Ones start condemning others and become cruel and punitive to eliminate wrongdoers. They generally get nervous breakdowns and depressions and attempt suicide while having depressive and obsessive-compulsive personality disorders.

Symbols

Ones are symbolized by the barking terrier animal. Moreover, the hardworking nature of ones is characterized by bees and ants. Ones are constantly building up and maintaining their own life as well as others' lives. Just like bees test all flowers and gather the best honey from all of them, similarly, ones bring out the best in others.

When it comes to the symbolic country, Ones are represented by Switzerland. They are clean and orderly just like the country and signify the virtually ideal democratic society of the nation. Switzerland is known for making precision watches and having a tranquil environment and flawless defense system.

Ones are represented by silver color, which is a clear, sober, and cool color. It signifies moonlight, which is derived from the sun, the highest ideal. The mild moonlight stands for growth and change in type one people.

Examples

Lucy van Pelt, the antagonist of Charlie Brown in 'Peanuts' belongs to type one. She is constantly trying to change the world, especially Charlie Brown, the eternal loser. Lucy wants to live in an ideal world where she can be happy. She craves for unconditional love, such as shown by her brother Linus towards her.

Some famous examples of type one include monk Martin Luther (1483-1546), Paul (a Pharisee), Confucius, Plato, Joan of Arc, Sir Thomas More, Pope John Paul II, Mahatma Gandhi, Nelson Mandela, Prince Charles, Margaret Thatcher, Kate Middleton, Jimmy Carter, Hillary Clinton, Michelle Obama, Osama bin Laden, Martha Stewart, George Bernard Shaw, Celine Dion, Harrison Ford, and Meryl Streep.

Personal Growth

Growth opportunities for Enneagram one personality type are as follows:

1. Respect others' opinions

Ones should learn to accept their imperfections and others' opinions. Everyone has their own standards so do not judge people as per your standards and expectations. Your map is not the territory for others. You should see and respect the views of others in order to resolve conflicts.

In fact, your own wisdom can enrich when you consider others' perspectives as well. Accept the reality instead of judging and understand the subjectivity and grey areas in life. Inspire others by example and not through criticism.

2. Don't try to be perfect

You should chase excellence instead of perfection since everyone is imperfect and a work-in-progress. You do not have to be perfect always and you cannot control all things. Moreover, learn to relax and spend some time on yourself. If you don't achieve something, do not think that there will be disaster and chaos due to it. You might feel

that the salvation of the world only depends
on you but that that's not true and you know
it well.

3. Forgive yourself and others

Forgive yourself for your mistakes and then
try again. Your mistakes will make you a
better person. Moreover, forgive others when
they make mistakes. You are a good teacher
and can teach a lot of things to others but
don't expect that others will change
immediately. They would not be as objective
and self-disciplined as you. Plus, they might
know what is right but due to several reasons
are unable to change immediately. Be patient
as they might change in the future.

4. Don't be serious all the time and have fun

Laugh as you don't have to be serious at all
times. Do not take yourself very seriously and
laugh at yourself. Moreover, laughter is also
helpful for your repressed anger as it instantly
relaxes you. Play a little and find areas of your
lives that are freer, lighter, and offer
spontaneous creativity.

It is good to try to be good in everything you
do but there's nothing wrong with having fun

and enjoying the simple pleasures of life till you are not breaking any law or hurting anyone. Appreciate the beauty of life with all the imperfections and flaws.

5. Don't get angry easily

When you feel irritated, think if you are asking a lot from yourself as well as others. You easily get annoyed by all the wrong things others commit but your frustration will not help in any way. Moreover, your anger and harsh self-criticism on your failures will not help you grow. So, there is no point doubting yourself and being nervous and tense about it. This is just your superego undermining you.

Try on work on the above-mentioned things for yourself and others and you will see a lot of changes in yourself after a while. And, don't forget that you are worthy of love. Be with people who acknowledge your strengths and help you work on your weaknesses.

CHAPTER 10

Enneagram Type 2: The Helper

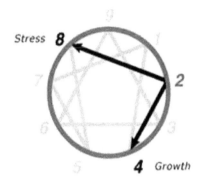

Enneagram Type 2 is named as the Helper. People of this type are characterized by selflessness. They prefer being the caring mentor for those around them.

True to their name they are ready to help anytime it is needed. This enneagram personality actively looks for ways and means to bring about a change for the better in other people.

The main personality traits in the helper include the tendency to help, provide, self-sacrifice, and empathize with others. Enneagram Helpers are emotionally aware and possess a generous nature. They try to find opportunities that can make a change in the lives of others.

They have this innate need to bend backwards to help others in order to be accepted in society. And they expect a similar sacrifice from others and when this does not happen, they are hurt deeply. Or, their struggles to acquire or sustain the affection of others can cause burnout or other related psychosomatic issues. Such issues arise due to the innate feeling of worthlessness that helpers have.

The core nature of the Enneagram helper is to shower affection on others and give to the society in some way to improve it for the better. While it is true that the helpers can go beyond their capacity to help others to the extent that they neglect their own needs, there is still hope for them. They have the capability of conscious thoughts and feelings, which remains the ultimate self-development goal they are able to reach.

Overview

Twos are warm-hearted, sincere in their affection, and empathetic. They act in a friendly way, and besides their generous and self-sacrificing nature, they are also people-pleasing. They tend to flatter others and are sentimental.

While their intentions are well-meant and try to be affectionate to others, they can easily slide into people-pleasing attitude just to satisfy their craving to be needed by others. This leads to issues like possessiveness and failure to understand their true needs.

In short, the two are

- Altruistic and unselfish in their attitude and shower love on others.

- They belong to the Heart Triad, which also has Enneagram types four and three.

- The most basic fear they have is being considered unworthy or unwanted

- The thing they desire most is to feel loved by others

- A one-winged Enneagram Helper is a Servant

- Three-winged Enneagram is a host or hostess.

- Flattery is the ego fixation trait in them

- Their one true vice is pride.

- Humility is a commendable virtue they possess

- When in the self-development mode, Twos integrate with the individualists or Fours

- When stressed twos disintegrate into the challenger or Eight type

Typical values you can find in the helper

- Kindness
- Empathy
- Altruism
- Togetherness

- Friendship and family

Why Twos Are Named As Helpers

The Helper terminology is assigned to the twos as they genuinely want to help others. In some unhealthy twos, they just perceive themselves as being helpful.

The motivation behind their helpful attitude is their belief that their generosity and helping nature makes them feel they live a meaningful and rich life. The goodness they extend to others makes them feel happy and valued.

Healthy Twos

When in a healthy state, Twos do not hold on to the belief that they have to keep doing everything they can for those around them. Instead, they first take care of their own self and even seek help from others to solve their issues.

However, their innate generosity in relation to energy and time is the same. This attitude makes them feel rested, humble, grateful, and healthy. Imagination, creativity, and introspection are also part of their traits, whey they are in a healthy condition.

In their balanced and healthy state, Twos attract people to them. Their glowing nature warms people's hearts. This includes the attentive and appreciative way they behave towards others. They help others identify their strengths, which they were not aware of before.

In a nutshell, a healthy two is like an ideal human being that everyone aspires to be. Someone who is helpful, empathetic, motivating, has endless patience, and is always ready to help while knowing the right time to leave things as they are. Healthy Twos warm our hearts as they show how a true human being can be.

Average Twos

In their average state, Twos are very devoted, helpful, and caring towards others. But, they tend to overthink about how others see them. This overanalyzing attitude makes them try hard to please others. In an extension of this attitude, they flatter and also become overbearing. Passive-aggressive behavior is formed in twos in this average state when they suspect that they are exploited by others.

Twos in Transitional State (Average to Unhealthy)

In the transitional phase, Twos show their inability to be an independent and self-loving person. Instead, they are dominated by the darker side of their personality, which includes self-deception, pride, interfering in other people's lives, and being manipulative to make themselves feel good. This changing phase stems from the fear that Twos have of not being worthy of the love of others. This is seen in Enneagram Threes and Fours too.

The three Enneagram types have the same underlying fear of being undervalued. This makes them overexert themselves to gain acceptance of others. In the transitional state, they project an incorrect image of being overgenerous and sacrificing.

They act like they do not want anything in return for their good deeds, but in truth have huge expectations. They also harbor several unattained emotional needs. In their craving to feel valued by others, Twos are ready to sacrifice their own needs over that of others.

However, this self-sacrificing attitude only makes them more miserable. They become resentful and angry and try to hide these feelings. However, these feelings explode in different ways damaging their relationships and making all their claims of love and generosity false.

Unhealthy Twos

In their unhealthy state, Twos are afraid that people will shun them due to their manipulative behavior. They perceive others as being selfish, as they feel that they have been exploited. This makes them feel exhausted and they suffer burn out. They can end up being in codependent or toxic relationships. They feel victimized as they believe that all their efforts to please and help others were futile.

Development Levels

Healthy Development Levels

Level 1

When in their best development levels Twos are very humble, altruistic, and selfless. They feel honored to be of help to others

Level 2

In this level, Twos feel compassionate and empathetic towards others. They show care and concern for others and their needs. Other traits they develop include warm-heartedness, sincerity, forgiveness, and thoughtfulness

Level 3

In this level, Twos are appreciative and motivate others. They have a positive outlook and consider serving as an important part of their makeup, but also care for their own needs. They show generosity, nurturing, and giving. In short, they turn into a truly caring person.

Average Development Levels

Level 4

Twos feel the need for affection from others. This triggers a people-pleasing attitude. They become over demonstrative and friendly and are brimming with good intentions. This results in flattery, approval, and attention. They value love the most and constantly speak about it.

Level 5

Twos in this level act intrusive and are excessively intimate. Their craving to feel needed makes them interfere in the affairs of others and control them. They demand others to rely on them. When they give to others, they do it expecting something in return. They are possessive and enveloping turning into a codependent and self-sacrificing individual who always puts the needs of others first. This wears them totally and creates a deep-seated need in them that is never fulfilled.

Level 6

Twos start feeling more and more satisfied and significant about themselves. They think they are essential, which is an overrated belief on their part. They become arrogant, condescending, and domineering. They martyr themselves for those around them.

Unhealthy Development Levels

Level 7

In this level, Twos turn into self-serving and controlling individuals. They make others feel guilty by pointing to what they owe them. They use medications and food to attract sympathy.

Demeaning and undermining behavior is rampant. They are unaware of their own aggressive and domineering behavior.

Level 8

They act coercive and domineering. They feel that they deserve whatever they are looking for from others such as sexual favors, money, etc.

Level 9

Twos in this level, resort to excuses on their bad behavior as they feel that they are the victim and turn into angry and resentful

beings. Chronic aggressive behavior causes
health issues and even results in factitious or
histrionic disorder.

Symbols

When Two move in the direction of
stress/disintegration, they acquire dominating
and aggressive traits at Eight. But when
moving towards growth direction, the self-
deceiving and prideful Twos turn into
emotionally knowledgeable and self-nurturing
just as healthy Fours.

Examples

Common occupations of Twos

- Caretaker
- Counselor
- Teacher
- Psychologist
- Nurse

Common hobbies that the Helper takes up
include gardening, socializing, cooking,
volunteering, and counseling.

Good examples of Twos in the prominent
position include Pope John XXIII, Byron

Katie, Paramahansa Yogananda, Nancy Reagan, Stevie Wonder, Luciano Pavarotti, Elizabeth Taylor, Danny Glover, Eleanor Roosevelt, Martin Sheen, Barry Manilow, and Dolly Parton.

Personal Growth

Gender perspective

It is common for Twos to wrongly categorize themselves if they do not play a clear helper part professionally. They will be unable to identify their exact role in helping others. This is more so in case of male Twos, as generally, they do not receive similar rewards socially as a female Two would receive.

Thus, male Twos incorrectly categorize as Threes or Ones and with Twos as their wings. In the case of females, nearly all have some or other dynamics related to the Two category. This is because these traits have been instilled in them socially.

Female Nines are often wrongly typecast as Twos, especially when they are young mothers of toddlers. However, While Twos have a strong awareness of their value and are proud, Nines are humble and self-effacing. The general recommendations that foster personal growth in Twos include:

1. Self-care first

The key factor you have to consider as a Helper is that you have to put yourself first. Why?

Only when you take care of your innermost needs and feel content can you be free of resentments and frustration.

You can respond to those around you in a calm and prepared manner when you are not worried about meeting your needs. And last but not least, taking care of yourself is the most practical thing that can help you reach your desires and goals.

2. Motives matter

Helping others is a virtue that is highly commendable in any individual. But before you venture into doing good deeds you have to be clear about what your motive is. If you go in expecting others to applaud or appreciate your help, you are in for a big disappointment.

Twos are at high risk of becoming codependent in their love relationships and almost always their partner will not provide what they really need.

3. Help when needed

Being a generous and giving person, you may wish to cater to several needs of others. But before you do, make sure they need your help. Although one of your traits is knowing what others need intuitively, it does not imply that they really want their needs to be satisfied with your help or in the way you want to help.

To avoid this, learn to communicate what your intentions are, and if they say no to your assistance accept it. If a person rejects your help, it does not imply that he or she is rejecting or does not like you.

4. Avoid boasting about the help you give

It may be tempting to tell about your good deeds to everyone and the people you assist. Remaining others of the help they received from you may make them uncomfortable or embarrassed. It can damage your relationship and leave you and others unsatisfied.

Instead, let your good deeds speak for themselves. If others remember your good deeds and express their gratefulness accept it. But don't go asking for it.

5. Recognize the affection of others

It is important that you learn how to identify the good wishes and affection that others show you. This is because different people have different ways to show their affection and that they truly care for you.

When you are able to identify this easily, you can comfort yourself with the fact that you are loved genuinely. This will help you acquire more of the healthy and beneficial traits, instead of the darker ones. And, remember that love is omnipresent. It is up to you to find it and be receptive.

CHAPTER 11

Enneagram Type 3: The Achiever

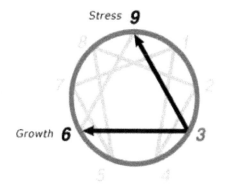

Ennagram Type 3 is given the name
Achiever. As the name implies Threes
value achievement. They are
competitive and hence place significance on
results, efficiency, image, and recognition.
Threes try to reach the pinnacle of success in
their specific field. They are ready to adapt to
changes and are flexible if it accomplishes
their goals.

Others view Threes as highly principled,
receptive, and hard-working persons. They
adapt to their surroundings or situations easily

and are ambitious. They are enthusiastic persons and love to set goals and achieve them.

They are seen as positive signs of integrity and hope. In the unhealthy phase, Threes show excessive cravings for accomplishment and are inconstant, and stress more on self-importance. This attitude is due to the value they attach to their deeds, instead of their own self.

The main strengths of Threes include their drive to succeed in their goals. They also motivate and encourage others to succeed. Practical approach, efficiency, confidence, and charisma are other strengths of Threes.

The weaknesses of Threes include being seen as overly ambitious, insensitive, inability to accept failure, and placing too much significance on self-image.

The brief description of threes is as follows:

- The basic fear Threes feel is of not being valued

- Basic desire in Threes is being seen as worthwhile and valuable

- Two-winged Achiever is The Charmer

- Four-winged Achiever is The Professional

Overview

At their basic level, Threes are sophisticated and polished. They have a love for finer things and are not afraid of striving to achieve them. Thus, you can see them well-dressed, determined, and smart.

Threes possess enormous productive capacity and fix exacting standards for themselves. They break their own records of success and are admired by people for their dedication and high-level performance. They are also an inspiration for others to follow in their steps.

The main objective of Threes is to receive accolades and commendations for their work, discoveries, and achievements. And true to their nature, achievers are perpetually busy with an always brimming schedule.

Core values in the Achiever

Threes have the following core values:

- Status

- Accolades

- Recognition

- Relentless self-improvement

- Goal-driven

- Achievement

- Productivity

In short, wasted time is not in the vocabulary of the Achievers.

How Threes are motivated

Threes are motivated by their feelings of desire, fear, longing, and weaknesses as follows:

While Threes strengths are their fear of being seen as a failure and desire of achieving status, their weakness is the effort the make-believe effort they put in to make them look respectable.

Their core fear is of being seen as incompetent, worthless, ineffective, and as a failure. The desire to be seen as a successful, respected, valuable, and admired person motivates their every action.

Deceit and truth embellishment are two core weaknesses found in Threes. They believe that what they show to the world is an image of themselves and not their true self. The personality that the world admires is just a polished cover they make for themselves.

Healthy Threes

In their healthy state, the Achievers do not need constant admiration or accolades from others. They are confident about the love of others and have high self-esteem. So, they do not find the need to strive for the approval of others.

Threes are highly skilled individuals and excel in situations where the resolution of problems, goal setting, efficiency, and productivity are needed.

And, in a healthy state, they accomplish great things not for their own good but for others. They do not feel the craving for the approval of others. Instead, they motivate others to improve their values, work, and achievements.

Threes in a healthy state are well-liked and act as role models in their society, culture, and family. They achieve several distinguishing feats in whatever field they are in such as acting, modeling, writing, politics, religion, and more. Their performance brings them positive attention and high praise.

In short, healthy threes trust and believe that they are children of Christ and hence are valuable. They do not stress the importance of their capability to build an impressive persona or image, but rather put their trust in Christ.

They are sincere, accepting, and kind. Although they aim to be competent and achieve the high goals they serve as an inspiration and also connect with their community in various helpful ways.

Average threes

Average Threes are not as confident as their healthy counterparts. They believe less about being of great value and their trust in Christ is not as pronounced. This waning belief makes them strive to earn the approval of others.

They alienate themselves from their core feelings and values and become susceptible to deceit, falseness, and self-deception.

They work hard to become an admired, successful, and well-respected person. To do this, they overexert and over-focus on every facet of their life including professional, family, work, health, and more.

In short, in the average phase, Threes aim high but do not reach their goals as they doubt their own ability. They are constantly worrying about losing their standing in society. They try very hard to compete with others and impress those around them. And they also try to make their grandiose claims true.

Unhealthy Threes

In the unhealthy state, Threes believe that their entire value relies on them being a successful and well-accomplished person. They put more importance on the opinions others have about them. They no longer place their trust in Christ and being his valued disciple. They forget their true nature and start creating a false image and accomplishments to receive love and approval from others. They refuse to acknowledge that what they are doing is wrong. And they also avoid revealing anything about themselves that can tarnish their image in front of others.

Threes are not considered as emotional people, and they believe that their performance is affected when they let in emotions. So, they often replace their feelings with practical action.

The unhealthy state of Threes is mainly because they have shunned their feelings and failed to manifest their authentic or core values. Since they work towards success and accomplishment single-mindedly, they end up paying dearly for their lack of emotional attachment. As a result, they feel empty and defeated. They try to hide their feelings of insecurity from others and even hurt others who reject them.

Development Levels

Healthy Development levels

Level 1

In this development level, Threes are healthy and exhibit their best traits, which include authenticity and self-acceptance. They act benevolently and are gentle. Modesty, charitability, and humor are other outstanding traits seen in this level.

Level 2

Threes at this level show high energy and are self-confident. Their self-esteem is very good and they recognize their true value. These qualities make them behave in a gracious, desirable, and attractive way. They are also easy to adapt to any situation.

Level 3

In this level, Threes aspire intensely to enhance their achievements. This results in them acquiring ideal qualities admired by one and all. Their success serves as an inspiration to others.

Average Development levels

Level 4

In this average development level 4, Threes are worried about their work and as a result, focus fanatically towards achieving their goals. In this stage, they are terrified of failure and keep comparing their achievements and improvements with that of others.

The average Threes in their development stage turn into social climbers and career-oriented persona striving to be the best in everything they set out to do.

Level 5

Threes in this level are conscious about how others perceive them. Thus, they try to act in a way that others expect them to behave and also try to do things that will make them a successful person among the rest.

They are efficient and pragmatic, which is well and good, but they act in a premeditated way thus disconnect their inner feelings in their efforts to present a polished front. This leads to issues in credibility, inaccuracy, and intimacy.

Level 6

Threes in this development level look to create an impressive personality by boasting about their

accomplishments constantly.
They are narcissistic and have inflated beliefs about their own strengths and skills. They are seductive and exhibitionistic. And, they feel jealous about the accomplishment of others.

Unhealthy Development Levels

Level 7

The Achievers in this unhealthy development level are afraid of failing in their endeavors. They fear humiliation and to avoid it they turn into opportunistic and exploiting individuals. They are ready to go to any extent to reach the success and recognition they crave for.

Level 8

Threes at this level try to hide their errors and faults by being devious and dishonest. They turn into havoc creating betrayers ready to sabotage the efforts of others in order to be successful. They are inordinately jealous of all achievements made by others.

Level 9

This level brings out the worst traits in the Achievers as they turn vindictive. They hate seeing others be happy. Whenever they perceive something as symbolic of their shortcomings, they destroy it.

Thus, Threes resort to psychopathic behavior and are in danger of acquiring Narcissistic personality conditions at their worst state.

Symbols

When Threes start moving towards disintegration (stress) direction, they become apathetic and disengaged as they reach Nine. But when they move in the direction of growth /integration, Threes turn into cooperative individuals from being deceitful and vain. And thus, are like healthy state Sixes.

Examples

Popular careers chosen by the Achievers include actor, entrepreneur, social media specialist, journalist, and Brand Ambassador. In their free time, Threes display their talents in different ways. They either hone their existing talents or develop new and unique talents.

Some common hobbies that Threes take up include competitive sports, dancing, developing talents, planning, and singing.

Some great personalities belonging to Enneagram Type 3 include Augustus Caesar, Tony Blair, Bill Clinton, Arnold Schwarzenegger, Muhammed Ali, Michael Jordan, Oprah Winfrey, Tiger Woods, Elvis Presley, Taylor Swift, Tom Cruise, Demi Moore, Anne Hathaway, Ryan Seacrest, Will

Smith, O.J. Simpson, Deepak Chopra, Mitt Romney, and Carl Lewis.

Personal Growth

In order to reach personal growth, Threes should strive to follow the below suggestions:

Be Honest

When it comes to actual development as an Achiever, you have to learn to be honest about your feelings to yourself and others.

As an achiever, it is normal to be image-conscious but if you start boasting about your own prowess, it can turn self-deceptive. You can lose connection with your true self and your purpose in life. Others too react to your actions by seeing you as uncaring, opportunistic, and insincere.

Avoid attempting to show yourself as an important person. Your appeal lies in your authentic behavior and accomplishments, and not in your boasting or exaggerating your achievements.

Build strong relationships

As a Three, a strong and lasting relationship is possible only when you are cooperative and care for others. Even if you are busy, try to spend some time with someone you like. A few minutes talking to them or appreciating their efforts is sufficient. This will help you connect with the person and gain you a faithful friend or partner. You will also start feeling better.

Find time to relax

In your fanatic rush to become successful and achieve your goals, you can end up being burnt out or exhausted. You can also drive others around you to a frustrated state.

While it is good to be ambitious and develop your skills, productivity, and career, as the saying goes, all work and no play makes you a dull person.

So, take some time to relax. This will help you distress and rejuvenate. You can reconnect with your goals in a more energetic way after taking short breaks. Your perspective too would improve with a relaxing time.

Social participation

Your personality has the capacity to achieve greater heights if you focus some of your energy on projects that are not concentrated on your development alone. By cooperating with your colleagues, friends, or others, and helping them in reaching a common goal, you are going beyond your personal space. This is when you can find a genuine identity and self-value.

Be emotionally invested

Instead of shutting out your feelings totally, as the average Threes try to do, avoid doing things just to get the approval of others. Try to view a situation in an objective way instead of what others would expect you to do in the situation.

Don't avoid negative issues or dismiss them, especially if they are related to your shortcomings or errors. When you spend time in identifying and relating to your core values, you are truly able to achieve great things without any of the malicious attachments such as narcissism, jealousy, etc.

CHAPTER 12

Enneagram Type 4: The Individualist

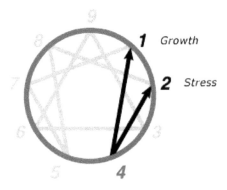

Individualists or Fours, as the name implies, are unique in their choice of lifestyle, interests, creativity, fashion, etc. Individualists are endearing and romantic persons with an offbeat personality and a relentless drive to know their true purpose in life.

They place more importance on creating new things than consuming them. Their time is spent on reflection of past experiences and emotions, which they use to hone their creativity. Fours use intangible concepts and tangible objects to recognize their true selves and nature. They use different modalities, philosophies, and ideologies for forming a unique lifestyle.

The pursuit of the inner self that includes conscious and the unconscious aspects helps them produce creative things that are not affected by external influences. They sail alone and are free-spirited persons who rule only by the values that they believe in. On the flip side, Fours deal with plenty of fear put in them by their peers, persons of authority, or teachers from childhood.

Fours are influenced by peak experiences and in their adolescent stage, they find it difficult to anchor themselves to their surroundings. They are forever searching for the purpose of their existence. When they are in a flowing state, they feel happy. As they enter adulthood, they are more aware of their identity and role in their society.

Overview

Healthy Fours

Healthy Fours are confident of their own self. They do not let feelings of worthlessness affect their thoughts and actions. The Fours are typically ruled by their feelings and imagination.

Thus, they end up being creative, inspiring, sensitive, and articulate persons. Or they can be elitist, self-absorbed, and moody.

The main characteristic traits in Fours include the following:

- The core fear felt by Fours is being defective, emotionally abandoned, inadequate, and unimportant.

- The core desire that rules Individualists is being authentic, special, and unique

- The core weakness felt by Fours is the envy of others due to feelings of being flawed or lacking some important thing in themselves

Fours have the core longing to be seen as a unique, special, and well-loved being. In their healthy state, Fours are on a roll creating path-breaking things and work towards the betterment of the society. They are considered as concept creator and inspire innovative thoughts in others.

They are instrumental in bringing about a grand shift in trends in all creative spheres including fashion and art. Fours are known for their innovative concepts and can reinvent newer works through their past experiences. The growth of Fours from childhood to adulthood is seen as a metamorphosis, where they attain self-acceptance and emerge as confident persons soaring high.

In the average state, Fours use their creativity to relax. They are inspired by mingling with similar thinking people and use such people to support their creative skills. They are introspective, intense, and can at times disregard the feelings of others to achieve what they set out to do.

Fours are very expressive artistically and also self-absorbed. This makes them create inspirational things and to form a unique identity for them.

Average Fours

In their average state, Fours can become hypersensitive to any criticism from others but remain firm in their beliefs. They start expecting flattery and praise in response and are offended, if their work is copied or when others have experiences that are similar to them.

Imagination is used in hordes by average Fours to fuel their mood and creativity. They can lead fantasy lives but are afraid of being proactive.

They often dream about others understanding them and accepting them. Fours are plagued by feelings of melancholy, self-consciousness, being misunderstood, and envy.

Unhealthy Fours

In an unhealthy state, Fours are afraid of not doing anything and failing to keep up with their ideals. Their drive to have a good self-image makes them shun those that do not support their outlook. This makes Fours angry, isolated, and depressed. They try to counter these negative feelings by losing themselves in a dream world.

The depressed and moody state makes Fours fragile and they start ruminating. This blocks their creative skills and in the extreme unhealthy state, they can lose touch with the real world and begin addicted to substances.

Their search for the missing part in them makes them take convoluted and wrong paths resulting in failures and self-damaging patterns and behaviors. Fours in their unhealthy state resort to the belief that they are broken and this spikes their stress levels. And, some desperate Fours can even cut off contact with the outer world like deleting their social media profiles and more.

Challenges for Fours

The most significant challenge faced by Fours is letting go of their past emotional experiences. They keep pondering over their failures and negative emotions. They become attached to disappointment and craving that they find it difficult to identify the positive things they have in life.

When Fours do not shake off the feeling that something is broken inside them, they will not be able to see the positive attributes they have. To recognize their strengths, they would have to lose the negative and depressed mindset and keep at bay their core fear of not being worthy. However, there is hope for Fours when they learn that negativity is not all that they have and when the bad feelings fall apart, they can truly act in a positive way.

Development levels

Healthy development levels

Level 1

Fours are very creative when it comes to expressing their personal feelings, and when relating to the universe. They are focused on self-renewing, regenerating, and being inspired. They have the skill to turn their past experiences into valuable present works.

Level 2

In this level, Fours are introspective and search for their inner self. They become aware of their inner thoughts and feelings and are as a result intuitive and sensitive to themselves and those around them. Compassion, tactfulness, and gentleness are traits found in Fours in this development level.

Level 3

This level has Fours being very individualistic, personal, and honest in an emotional way. They also possess a critical view of life and their inner self. Humor and serious traits are present in them and they exhibit emotional strength while being vulnerable.

Average Development Levels

Fours in this development level have a romantic outlook of life and take to artistic creativity.

They use their creative skills to develop and prolong their own emotions. They also try to boost their reality using impressive imagination, fantasy, and passionate feelings.

Level 5

Fours take all things seriously and internalize their feelings. They do this to be connected with their emotions. They turn into introverted, self-absorbed, hypersensitive, and moody persons.

They are also self-conscious and shy, which leads to their inability to be spontaneous or think innovatively. They try to safeguard their self-image by withdrawing from socializing. The alone time is for sorting their conflicting feelings.

Level 6

Individualists consider themselves as a class apart from others. This makes them believe that they need not live like others. They become dreamers and act in a decadent, disdainful, and even sensual way.

They like living in a world created by their own fantasies. They envy the achievements of others and pity themselves. This causes self-indulgence and they turn into ineffective, unproductive, and impractical persons.

Unhealthy Development Levels

Level 7

Fours are angry with themselves and inhibit their growth when their dreams fail to materialize. They feel depressed and isolate themselves and others. They become frozen emotionally and block all their feelings. They are prone to fatigue and inertia due to the shame they feel of their ineptitude.

Level 8

Fours are tortured by self-inflicted thoughts that reproach, spew hatred, and contempt on themselves. They develop morbid thoughts and all types of feelings are torture for them. Fours hoist blame on others and try to drive away those who want to assist them.

Level 9

Fours in this level are pushed to deep despair, hopelessness, and turn into self-damaging behavior. They take up substance abuse to escape from negative emotions. In their worst developmental stage, they can suffer an emotional breakdown and even commit suicide. This stage of Fours is connected to Narcissistic personality condition, avoidance, and depression.

Symbols

The Fours in the Enneagram symbol when moving towards stress or disintegration direction, the aloof Fours turn contrary and stay at Two. But when they move in the growth or Integration direction, Fours that are emotionally imbalanced and envious turn into principled and objective just like Ones.

Examples

When Fours choose a career path they are attracted to jobs where they are able to express their creative skills and emotions to others and be an inspiration. Popular occupations that appeal to Fours include designer, actor, photographer, personal trainer, hairstylist, author, illustrator, counselor, artist, and activist.

In their free time Fours try to release their pent-up emotions via creative outlets. They deal with their emotional thoughts alone. In fact, some of the noted artists in history belong to Enneagram type Four. They are talented at working with varied mediums and exhibit a fascinating emotional spectrum with their work.

Common hobbies Fours like include reading, acting, journaling, watching movies, listening to music, and designing.

A few examples of popular Fours including Edgar Allen Poe, Tennessee Williams, Anne Rice, Judy Garland, Bob Dylan, Annie Lennox, Sarah McLachlan, Ingmar Bergman, Angelina Jolie, Nicolas Cage, Rumi, Chopin, Yukio Mishima, and Virginia Wolf.

Personal Growth

Growth opportunities for Fours are fostered when they recognize and redirect their self-centered objectives. Spending some time to ruminate over their strengths, and acknowledging that getting help from others is a good thing are things that can enhance the personal growth of Fours.

Fours are emotional and romantic when their partner strikes a deep-set connection with them. Relationships for Fours work only when they do not attempt to place impossible expectations or idealize their partners.

Here are a few recommendations that can help the Individualists to boost their personal growth, capitalize on their positive traits, and overcome their negative traits.

Listen to your feelings

While feelings can help you identify yourself, do not attach too much significance to your feelings. Equating your behavior with what you feel is a big mistake you can do as a Four. You need to recognize the negative and positive part of your feelings prior to acting upon them.

In general, Fours cannot distinguish between their self and their feelings. They also fail to recognize that negative feelings do not negate the presence of good feelings. What you need to understand is that your feelings are a window to your inner self at the present moment, but not a profound one.

Don't Procrastinate

When you put off doing things because you are not in a good mood, you will not be able to be as productive as you would like to be. Instead, commit yourself to contribute as much as you can to the good of others and yourself.

When you work consistently, it can create an environment that will help you recognize your talents and your own self. Being busy and productive will leave you with little time to procrastinate or wait for your creative inspiration to occur. In short, remain connected with reality to realize your dreams.

Shun negativity

Do not ponder on negative, resentful, or excessively passionate thoughts. Prolonged negative conversations with your own self are not real.

These do not drive you towards taking action. So, try to spend your time living every moment instead of spending it imagining the relationships and life you will lead.

Practice self-discipline

Good self-discipline is essential to remain healthy and live life with the individuality you aim for. To accomplish this, you have to allot time in your daily routine for exercise, a good diet, and sleep. This will act cumulatively and strengthen your body and mind.

Self-discipline can help in enhancing your individuality. Becoming addicted to drugs, alcohol, sensuality, excessive sexuality, and fantasies can be destructive for you.

Embrace positive thoughts

When you think positive thoughts, you will be able to develop self-confidence and self-esteem. Even if you are not ready to face a challenging task, use your positive thoughts to motivate yourself.

Fours in general are always afraid of falling apart but need to build the courage needed to stop putting off things. Regardless of how small you begin, throw your all into a task with full commitment so you are able to give your best to it.

CHAPTER 13

Enneagram Type 5: The Investigator

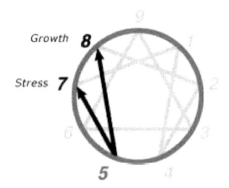

E nneagram Type Five is called The Investigator/Observer/Loner. The fives generally focus on assimilating knowledge and are high on intellectuality. Hence you will find fives as technical experts or scholars as they have good analytic skills and high perceptive sense.

Fives like to act independently and value their privacy. They perceive others as intruding with their lives. As Loners, Fives can easily stay detached from any emotional upheaval or pressure, which may free them, but leave them lonely.

Although Fives are intellectual persons, they find relationships and feelings a big challenge. For some, friends and family are significant, but they will still want their own time for focusing on their interests.

Fives need to find a balance between their habit of withdrawing from others and interacting with others, in spite of the effort bringing discomfort to them.

Fives are entranced by the world and the happenings around them. While they feel whatever events and people around them are intrusive, they also find them highly stimulating and enhancing their knowledge.

Fives feel a strong craving for knowledge as they believe that it helps them deal well with their lives and the people around them. Thus, they are forever preparing themselves, thinking constantly, and assessing things. These efforts prevent them from living life fully.

They avoid emotional involvement and limit their needs. They make do with whatever resources they have and spend most of their waking time studying their environment and observing others without participating themselves.

Overview

Fives are curious, insightful, and alert individuals. They use their time on developing skills and complicated concepts. You can find fives as inventors, innovators, and independent thinkers. They are detached from others, but at the same time are intense and ready to act. Fives have issues with isolation and eccentricity.

Some common traits that fives have include

- At their very best, fives are visionaries and pioneers who are able to think innovatively and perceive things with a unique outlook.

- The most basic fear fives have is of being incapable, helpless, and useless

- Fives have the basic desire to be competent and skilled in whatever they do

- Fives with four-wings are termed Iconoclast and fives with six wings are termed as Problem Solvers.

- Fives have their main motivation to acquire knowledge and understand the world in their effort to make themselves face the challenges of the world effectively.

- The core strategies Fives use is secluding themselves in an inner world, limiting their needs and using up their resources in an economic way.

Healthy Fives

Healthy fives are very confident in facing life and are filled with knowledge. They are empathetic and insightful. As keen observers, Fives are capable of connecting with different personalities easily. They love sharing their knowledge with others and take delight in experimenting with concepts, artwork, inventions, and more.

As investigators, Fives are pioneers in their respective fields and regarded with respect for their intellectual contribution to society. They are able to perceive the most complex issues with precision and clarity.

Fives are capable of turning the impossible to easily achievable with their confident approach, innovative thinking, and unique concepts. They are experts in their field and share their discoveries with the world. They are able to get across even the most complex topics in an easy to understand way.

Average Fives

In the average state, Fives are worriers. They feel that the knowledge acquired by them is not sufficient to face the world. They focus intensely on their practice, study, and inner mind, and gather knowledge avidly. They detach themselves from others and focus on alternate realities and possibilities. With a big chunk of their time taken up in acquiring the knowledge, they have very little time left for taking action.

Investigator Fives are withdrawn and offbeat. They tend to keep some of their interests hidden from the world and hold themselves aloofly. They are experts in their chosen field and try to assimilate knowledge related to different virtual worlds as a means of escape from their routine and tedious life. They love to play strategic card or board games in their free time.

Unhealthy Fives

Unhealthy fives are mostly isolated, eccentric, and often do not relate themselves to the real world. They find solace in removing themselves from the real world. They find retreating into their mind keeps them stress-free. They perceive the world as a dark and dangerous place that they need to flee. They are obsessive about assimilating knowledge and go after knowledge to escape from incompetent and insecure feelings they have.

Fives thus cut all ties with the real world and develop a tunnel vision. Their views are radical and farfetched. They do not have the foresight or emotional sense needed to make them anchored to the present.

Fives in an unhealthy state often venture in heated fights without any clear concept on the topic. Thus, they may lose many friendships. Unhealthy Fives feel that they will fare better when they isolate themselves.

They are attracted to bizarre theories and show themselves as intellectually superior. Their superior attitude and aloofness chase away people making Fives bitter and misanthropic. They are easily fatigued and stressed, when they face a large group of strangers, and when faced with emotional situations or expressions. They are not good at meeting the needs of others and feel drained by overstimulation.

Enneagram Fives are faced with big hurdles in professional and personal relationships, when they are overwhelmed and when they make sensible decisions that end up affecting others. They also find it difficult to relate to the emotions of others.

On the romantic front, Fives are calm and helpful towards their partners, if the partner is patient and supportive, and provides them the space they need for developing their intellectual knowledge. However, when they are with an introverted individual, they need to spend time with their partner to make the relationship work. However, in general, Enneagram Fives find it difficult to engage in serious conversations. They cannot talk freely about their emotions and do not offer verbal appreciation or affirmation.

Development Levels

Healthy Development Levels

Level 1

Fives when they exhibit their best traits come across as highly perceptive individuals. They are open-minded visionaries involved in remarkable and path-breaking discoveries. Fives in this level are also innovative thinkers and are involved in inventing sophisticated concepts and techniques.

Level 2

In the second level, Fives are insightful and possess incisive/probing intelligence. They are curious and alert with the ability to focus single-mindedly. They also possess predictive skills and foresight. They have a keen sense of observation.

Level 3

In this level, Fives hone their special skills to perfection. They are passionate about acquiring knowledge and considered experts in their respective filed. Their creative, inventive, and innovative skills ensure their works are highly valuable and authentic.

However, owing to the high level of intelligence and single-minded focus they exhibit Fives also come across as idiosyncratic, whimsical, and independent.

Average Development Levels

Level 4

In this level, Fives have a calculated approach to the things they do. They refine and tweak their concepts in a detailed way. They spend their time collecting resources, practicing, preparing, and building designs. They hone their skills and become highly intellectual and most importantly challenge already established concepts.

Level 5

Fives in this level gradually detach themselves from the happenings around them as they get deeply engrossed in working out complicated ideas. Their preoccupation with their concepts and visions make them forget about reality.

Esoteric and off-beat concepts grab their attention and they stay in a world that is separated from the real world. Fives are intense and wound tight in this level.

Level 6

Fives become aggressive in this level and stubbornly oppose anything that intrudes on their personal vision or world. They are abrasive and very provocative. They take on radical and extreme views and are confrontational and skeptical.

Unhealthy Development Levels

Level 7

Fives in an unhealthy state become totally separated from the real world and turn reclusive. They act eccentrically. They hate confrontations and act in a very unstable manner. Social attachments are abhorred by Fives in this level and they continue to reject overtures from people around them.

Level 8

Fives get so deeply involved in their concepts that they over obsess about them and are even fearful of the ideas they form. They become delirious and are prone to several phobias and bizarre distortions.

Level 9

In the peak unhealthy levels, Fives try to seek relief from their obsessive and eccentric behavior by resorting to suicide or they cut contact with reality completely. They act in a highly self-destructive way. Deranged and schizophrenic Fives are prone to conditions such as Schizotypal and Schizoid Avoidant disorders.

Symbols

In the Enneagram circle, when Fives move in direction of stress/disintegration, they change into scattered and hyperactive levels when they reach Seven. But when Fives move in direction of growth/Integration, they turn into decisive and confident personalities like Eight.

Examples

Popular occupations that Fives prefer include researcher, scientist, architect, professor, and technical writer. Fives like to spend their free time honing their skills. They prefer memorization, exercise, contextual thinking, and creativity related projects.

Common hobbies Fives love include involving in sports, computers, learning new facts, video games or board games, and non-fiction books.

Famous personalities who exhibit traits of Enneagram Type 5 include Buddha, Stephen Hawking, Albert Einstein, Vincent Van Gogh, Agatha Christie, Bill Gates, Alfred Hitchcock, Mark Zuckerberg, Tim Burton, Jodie Foster, Julian Assange, Oliver Sacks, and Georgia O'Keeffe

Personal Growth

Fives can experience great improvement in their growth and development when they follow the following recommendations:

Be in touch with reality

While it is natural for you to possess exceptional talents and mental skills, you should avoid hiding behind your skills making them a trap that holds you from interacting with others normally.

So, closely observe your thought process and identify when your thoughts drag you away from reality. By being connected with the real world, you will remain anchored and use your skills in a good way.

Relaxation helps

With most of your waking time spent on accomplishing innovative, intense, and high skilled tasks, you can easily fall prey to stress and anxiety. Try to relax by taking up healthy and efficient habits like exercising, yoga, dancing, jogging, meditation, and more.

Biofeedback methods are good for channeling your abundant energy to create good things. Avoid resorting to drugs and alcohol to feel relaxed and to unwind.

Gain a Proper Perspective

You may find it difficult to prioritize or choose the right option from the numerous possibilities present. Being focused on your work can make you miss your perspective and your ability to accurately analyze a situation.

To avoid such a situation, you can seek advice from people whom you can depend on. This will give you the right perspective. However, Fives are not prone to easily trust others, which can pose a big hurdle.

Take decisive action

When you are engrossed in multiple projects however attractive they may be, it will not be possible for you to give your all to them. This is especially true when you have your focus on different topics like hobbies, games, etc. besides your main subject.

These can distract you from your true purpose. This can affect your confidence and self-esteem levels. To avoid this, you need to take decisive action. This will instill confidence in you than learning about certain facts or assimilating unrelated talents.

Find people you trust

Since Fives have difficulty in trusting people or showing their emotions openly, it can prevent them from having healthy relationships. To avoid this, you have to find at least a couple of friends that you trust implicitly.

And remember that having trusted friends does not prevent you from having conflicts with them. Every relationship has its own potential set of issues you have to deal with. Working out such conflicts is a healthy thing to do, instead of outright rejecting the relationships or isolating yourself.

CHAPTER 14

Enneagram Type 6: The Loyalist

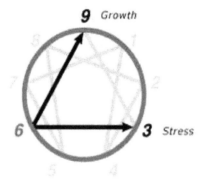

E nneagram Type Six is called The Loyalist. Sixes tend to reliable, responsible, hardworking, and trustworthy individuals that make for amazing 'troubleshooters'. They have the ability to foresee problems and cultivate cooperation.

As Fives are basically security-oriented, they can become quite defensive, anxious, and evasive. They can run on stress without letting others show. In their caution and indecisiveness, they can become reactive, rebellious, and defiant. They typically have issues with suspicion and self-doubt.

Fives at their best are courageous individuals that champion themselves and others. They orient themselves in the world based on the security-principle and as such wish to be supported by others and have reassurances.

From time to time, they may test others' attitudes towards them in order to fight anxiety and security. But this is just a way for Sixes to maintain a semblance of security. Their basic fear is being without guidance and support that they will go to any lengths to overcome. Their best versions are highly internally stable and self-reliant.

Overview

Of all the personality types, Sixes are termed the Loyalists for their loyalty to friends and their beliefs. They are also loyal to systems of thoughts, ideas, and beliefs – even the belief that the authorities or the 'status quo' should always be questioned and defied. In actuality, the beliefs of Sixes can be highly rebellious, anti-authoritarian, and revolutionary. As such, they will fight for their beliefs and their community harder than they will fight for themselves.

Some common traits of Sixes include the following:

- At their best, Sixes are internally stable and self-reliant

- Their most basic fear is being without guidance and support

- Their basic desire is to be supported and have security in life.

- Sixes with Five-Wing are termed 'The Defender' and with Seven-Wing as 'The Buddy'.

- The main motivations of Sixes include wanting to have security, fight anxiety and security, and have assurance and certitude.

Healthy Sixes

Healthy sixes are a paragon of self-reliance and stability. They will go out of their way to defend their community, beliefs, and friends against the odds. They are highly trustworthy and reliable individuals that make for great guides and friends. In their healthy state, they understand that the world is always changing and can be peaceful and serene in any circumstance.

Healthy sixes tend to have their beliefs in the self that leads them to positive thinking, courage, self-expression, and leadership. They are able to bring out strong emotional responses from others through love, affection, and trust. As such, Sixes tend to create stability and security in the world through loyalty, hard work, and perseverance.

Average Sixes

In the average state, Sixes oscillate between the influences that hit them the hardest. Because of their contradictory nature, regardless of what one says about them, chances are that the opposite is equally true. As such, they are fearful and courageous, strong and weak, aggressive and passive, defenders and provokers, trusting and distrusting, doubters and believers – and so on.

Once Sixes have sufficient support to face the anxieties of life, they are able to move forward with relative confidence. However, if that crumbles, they immediately become aware of their self-doubt and fear which reawakens their basic fear.

Unhealthy Sixes

Unhealthy Sixes struggle continually with the fear of abandonment and lack of support. They believe that their internal resources are not enough to handle life's challenges alone. This is the reason why they tend to cling to ideas, beliefs, and support structures outside themselves for survival.

Unhealthy Sixes have trouble contacting their inner guide which results in a lack of confidence in their own judgments. Being primarily in the Thinking Center, they tend to over-think and worry too much. It is the resultant fear of over-thinking that leads them to resist making important decisions.

Without a deep sense of support and inner guidance, Sixes are constantly struggling to find firm ground. Many Sixes come to believe that they do not have the internal resources necessary to handle life's challenges. As such, they rely increasingly on structures, beliefs, allies, and supports that lie outside themselves for assistance and guidance.

Development Levels

Healthy Development Levels

Level 1

At their best, Sixes becoming increasingly self-affirming and learn to trust themselves. They learn how to form interdependent and cooperative relationships that see both parties as equals. This symbiotic relationship leads to many good things in one's life and leads to mutual growth. Healthy Sixes' belief in self is a catalyst for true courage, leadership, positive thought, and creative self-expression.

Level 2

At this stage, Sixes are healthy and motivating enough to elicit strong emotional responses from other people. This is because they are very affectionate, lovable, appealing, and endearing. Their trust and loyalty make them a cherished asset in the world and their relationships with other people.

Level 3

At this stage, Sixes are individuals that are dedicated to beliefs and movements in which they firmly believe. This allows them to be at the helm of community development and growth. Their main traits of being responsible, trustworthy, and reliable come in especially handy here. Since they are hard-working and industrious, and can even sacrifice for others, they bring about a cooperative spirit in their community that helps them create a stable and secure world.

Average Development Levels

Level 4

At this stage, Sixes tend to invest their time and energy the things that they think will lead them to safety and stability. As they are organizing and structuring their lives, they look up to the authorities and their alliances for continual security and assurance. Sixes at this stage are always anticipating problems and are highly vigilant, lest their security falls from under their feet.

Level 5

At this stage, Sixes tend to be highly evasive, cautious, indecisive, ambivalent, and procrastinating. They react against others in a passive-aggressive way to resist having any more demands being made on them. When confronted, they become highly anxious, reactive, negative in their thoughts, and quite contradictory in the signals that they give. Their unpredictability is chiefly the result of their internal confusion.

Level 6

At this stage, Sixes become highly sarcastic and war-like. This they do to compensate for the loss of their securities, and can end up blaming others for their problems, even taking unreasonably tough stands towards those that they consider 'outsiders'. They exhibit tendencies quite opposite of their healthy counterparts, in that they become highly defensive and reactive, divide people strictly between friends and enemies, and are always on the lookout for threats to their security.

As such, Sixes become highly authoritarian even as they are afraid of authority, becoming highly suspicious of people, conspire against them, and instill fears into others so they own fears can be silenced.

Unhealthy Development Levels

Level 7

At this stage, Sixes feel that their sense of security is ruined. This makes them feel on edge, afraid, volatile, and self-effacing, which leads to feelings of acute inferiority. They tend to feel completely defenseless, which is why they look for figures of authority or beliefs to solve their problems for them. Sixes at this level can also be highly disparaging and tend to berate other people.

Level 8

At this stage, Sixes feel persecuted and believe them other people are after their lives. This is truly a sorry state in which Sixes act irrationally through fear and lash out at other people, projecting their fears onto everything that they see and come across. Sixes at this stage are characterized by violence and fanaticism.

Level 9

At this last stage, Sixes are at their worst. They look to escape punishments, even though their punishment is their own. As such they tend to be hysterical and self-destructive, verging even on suicide. Their behaviors are generally characterized by drug overdoses, alcoholism, and self-abasement. Their reactions take the form of passive aggression and their psyches can take on the forms of a paranoid personality disorder.

Symbols

When they move in the direction of stress and disintegration, Sixes end up becoming highly competitive arrogant at Three. On the other hand, when they move in the direction of growth and direction, the pessimism and fear of Sixes relax and turn into optimism, such as those of healthy Nines.

Examples

There are many jobs in which Sixes would excel. Some of the common career options that Sixes find themselves comfortable in include health and safety engineers, veterinarians, teachers, environmental scientists and specialists, police and detectives, and caretakers.

This works well for Sixes as they tend to anticipate problems and potential dangers in the environment. Since they are able to identify these potential hazards, they make great problem solvers. Their hobbies include volunteering, working in a non-profit organization, indulging in writing, painting, acting, and music – basically anything that they are able to do from the haven of their homes.

Some of the famous Type Six Personalities include Woody Allen, Mel Gibson, Tom Hanks, Jennifer Aniston, J.R.R. Tolkien, Sigmund Freud, Mark Twain, Malcolm X, Oliver Stone, Krishnamurti, Marilyn Monroe, Mark Wahlberg, David Letterman, Julia Roberts, George H. W. Bush, Richard Nixon, Ben Affleck, and Mike Tyson.

Personal Growth

Sixes can witness great growth in their personalities and character when they follow the developmental steps given below:

Coping with Anxiety

Know that there is nothing wrong with being anxious, as everyone gets anxious from time to time – much more than they may let on. Whenever you are getting anxious, learn to be present in it, look to explore it, and come to terms with it.

Try to work with your tensions in creative ways and do not turn to substances such as drugs and alcohol to get over them. If you are breathing properly and are aware of the anxiety, it can actually work for you and become an energizing factor that can make you more productive.

Inculcate Positivity

There is a tendency in you to get worked up when you are upset, so much so that you turn on others and blame them for things that have been your own doing. Always be aware of your negative attitude, your pessimism.

It results in a pattern of dark moods and negativity that you habitually project on reality. Whenever you think you are succumbing to self-doubt, make a conscious effort to look at the brighter side of things and know that no harm will come to you unless it comes from yourself.

Manage your Reactions

Whenever they are under stress, Sixes tend to overreact. If you want to overcome this habit, first learn to identify the things that make you overreact. Moreover, know that none of the things that you have feared have actually ever come true.

Even when things are actually as bad as you think, fear will only weaken you and debilitate you in dealing with those things. Even if you cannot manage external happenings, you are able to always manage your own thoughts and reactions.

Learn to Trust

There is no doubt that there are many people in your life that you care about and trust. If you do not have someone like this, you have to go out of your way to meet someone trustworthy and allow yourself to get close to the person. As a Six, it shouldn't be a problem for you to learn to trust people.

Even if at first you may feel like you are risking rejection, go ahead with it anyway, for the risk is worth it. Sixes have a gift of meeting people like themselves but when they are not sure of themselves, they can get in their own way and become afraid of making commitments. That is why it is important for Sixes to let people know how they feel about them from the get-go.

Assess your Fears

People generally think better of you than you think. Most of them are not out there to get you, even if you believe that to be the case. In reality, your fear of others should tell you more about your attitude towards other people than it does how others see you.

Take Responsibilities

As a Six, you are terribly afraid of accepting responsibility even when you are a highly responsible person by nature. This is mainly due to your fear of mistakes. You may fear that others may come after you for your mistakes. But, the fact of the matter is that people respect those who take responsibility, even if they make mistakes. If you pass the responsibilities to others, you may only end up alienating yourself and undermine the respect that others have for you.

Speak the Truth

Always be fair with others and let them know what you are thinking. If you fail to do this, others may see you as too defensive or decisive. Do not let falseness and lies cause conflict in your relationships with people.

Self-affirmation

As a Six, you want to feel safe and secure, but this is not possible unless you are secure within yourself. For that, self-affirmation is a necessary focus. That means you need to develop a belief in yourself as well as your own abilities that are realistic in nature.

The fact of the matter is that others won't believe in you unless you believe in yourself. To get started with it, you have to ground yourself in your body and allow your mind to get quieter. As this continues to happen, you become naturally confident and will feel supported by life.

Attitude towards Authority

Take a step back and assess your attitude towards authority. Do you always have a compulsively and reflexively rebel and resist authority? Do you look for it, trying to hide it naively just to avoid responsibility?

Most Sixes have highly charged issues with authority. To overcome this unconscious attitude, the first step is to become aware of it. The greater your awareness, the more you will be able to seek out the authority of your inner self.

Rely on Yourself

Finding a reliable source of guidance and support is always an issue for a Six. It is good to note that such sources are viable only up to a point and cannot provide lifelong stability that you are looking for. Nothing can be a substitute for your true nature for it alone can provide a sense of solidity and constant reliability in the world. You can be grateful for such sources of support in your life but it is better not to depend on yourself.

CHAPTER 15

Enneagram Type 7: The Enthusiast

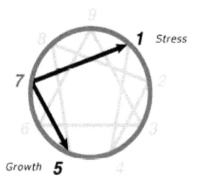

Sevens are a highly spirited breed. Their spontaneity is unparalleled as is their versatility and optimism. For these reasons they are highly extroverted individuals who find great joy and in social company. They are very playful and at the same time practical. They are multi-potentialities, meaning they have multiple talents.

Sometimes they may misapply their talents and end up becoming scattered and undisciplined. Though they are constantly on the lookout for new and exciting experiences, this same trait can also distract and exhaust them.

Their main problems come with being impatient and impulsive. But when Sevens are at their best, they are highly focused on their goals, are appreciative and satisfied, sharing their joyous self with others.

Overview

Sevens are called The Enthusiasts since they are innately enthusiastic about anything and everything that catches their attention. They approach their lives with a sense of adventure, a highly optimistic curiosity. They are like kids at a theme park, looking at the world with wide-eyed anticipation, eagerly waiting to jump on the rides and experience life.

Though they are in the Thinking Center, Sevens do not appear to be so since they are highly practical individuals that have multiple projects going on at any given time. Their attitude can well be described as a kind of brazen nerviness, as is evident by their energy levels.

Some common traits of Sevens include the following:

- The basic desire of Sevens is to be completely satisfied and content.

- Sevens' basic fear is being deprived or experiencing pain.

- Sevens' key motivation is to maintain freedom and happiness, experiencing everything worthwhile, and keeping them occupied and excited.

- Sevens with Six-wing are termed 'The Entertainer' while with Eight-Wing they are termed 'The Realist'.

- At their Best, Sevens are focused on worthwhile goals that keep them satisfied and joyous.

Healthy Sevens

Sevens, when they are healthy, are extremely exuberant and upbeat. They have the innate gift of being abundant with vitality which makes them highly optimistic in their outlook. They have a desire to participate fully in their lives and live each day to its full potential.

Sevens have agile minds which makes them fast learners. They are able to absorb information and learn new skills exceptionally fast. They have amazing dexterity and mind-body coordination, the unique combination of which truly makes them a renaissance person.

Sevens are naturally good-humored and cheerful and do not take themselves too seriously. When they are balanced within themselves, they affect everyone around them through their enthusiasm and unbridled joy.

Average Sevens

Given their highly active and enthusiastic approach, Sevens tend to engage in multiple projects at any given time. They move rapidly from one idea to the next which, though gives them good at brainstorming and synthesizing ideas, can make them get scattered. Although Sevens are not exactly high-browed intellectuals, they can be widely read and verbose.

Sevens have anticipatory thinking, meaning they foresee events and are able to generate ideas on the go. They favor activities that excite their minds which, in turn, end up generating more ideas and things to think about.

Sevens are borne along with life by their spontaneity and excitement. But, this can also create a lot of problems for them especially when they are not careful. As they can pick up multiple skills with relative skill, it can become difficult for them to decide exactly what they want to do with themselves. As such, they may not always value their abilities the way they would have if they had to struggle for them.

Unhealthy Sevens

In their unhealthy state, Sevens are out of touch with the support of the inner nature. Without their inner guide, they tend to get quite anxious in life. Unhealthy Sevens feel that they cannot make the right choices that would be beneficial to themselves as well as others.

Sevens try to cope with their anxiety in a few ways. They may try to keep themselves occupied with projects and future ideas all the time which keeps their negative feelings away from conscious awareness. Since their thinking is tied to their physical activity, they may be impelled to be on the move continuously which is another way by which sweep their problems under the carpet.

Sevens try to manage the loss of their inner guide through the method of 'trial and error'. This means that they will try everything to know what works best for them. In actuality, on a deeper level, they do not think they will ever find the things that they want in life.

As Sevens try to speed up their pursuit of the things that they believe will provide them with satisfaction, they end up making worse choices, which makes them unsatisfied, and their attempts become futile.

As such, Sevens can end up becoming frustrated and enraged as their emotional, physical, and financial resources begin to run out. Unhealthy Sevens may end up, over time, ruining their health, finances, relationships, and career in their search for happiness which is a tragic state of affairs for any individual.

Development Levels

Healthy Development Levels

Level 1

At their best, Sevens are able to assimilate their experiences deeply which makes them truly appreciative and grateful for the things that they have. They are inspired by the simple wonders of life, which makes them joyous and ecstatic in life. As such, they can be deeply rooted in spiritual reality and life's goodness.

Level 2

At this stage, Sevens are not only excitable and enthusiastic but also highly responsible. Since Sevens are an extroverted type, they immediately respond to stimuli and find most things invigorating. Their wealth of sensations and experiences makes them lively, resilient, eager, vivacious, and cheerful.

Level 3

Sevens at this level are healthy enough to easily accomplish multiple things. Their multi-potentialities allow them to harness their talents and synthesize them into coherent ideas. Sevens are prolific individuals who are very industrious, practical, and their energies between projects bounce off each other.

Average Development levels

Level 4

At this stage, Sevens are very restless. Due to their rising restlessness, they are driven to find more options and choices that are available to them. Though with multiple experiences, they become wise in the ways of the world and remain adventurous, they are not as focused. They are always looking for new things and experiences, and keeping up with the latest fads is important to them.

Level 5

Sevens at this stage cannot discriminate easily what they really want. Being hyperactive, they are unable to say 'no' to things, throwing themselves forever into activities. Sevens are uninhibited and do and say whatever comes to their mind. They fear boredom and would rather fill up the silences and the stillness with ideas, actions, and projects.

Level 6

At this stage, Sevens are prolific consumers. They will indulge in all sorts of excesses. This makes them self-centered, avaricious, materialistic, and greedy, for they are unable to become satisfied. Sevens can even become pushy and highly demanding of other people, even though it doesn't in the least give them any form of contentment.

Unhealthy Development Levels

Level 7

In their desperation to allay their anxieties, Sevens at this stage become infantile and impulsive. They become addicted to things and let their dissatisfaction lead them to excesses. Sevens end up becoming depraved escapists and their actions become abusive and offensive.

Level 8

At this stage, Sevens are in a rage to get away from themselves. To that end, they will act impulsively, have erratic mood swings, mania, and go out of control. They feel incapable of dealing with their anxieties and frustrations, which makes them feel worthless and out of sync with reality.

Level 9

At their worst, Sevens are all but spent. Their health and energy give way to depression and despair. They may become claustrophobic and indulge in self-destructive behaviors. Sevens at their worst are at a higher risk of suicide due to their impulsive nature. Their worst usually corresponds to bipolar and histrionic personality disorder.

Symbols

When Sevens move in the direction of stress and disintegrated, their scattered selves turn into highly critical perfectionists at One. On the other hand, when they move in the direction of growth and integration, they become much more focused and fascinated by life, similar to healthy Fives.

Examples

Sevens tend to have multiple talents and their vigor and vivaciousness allow them to pick up new things with relative ease. Some of the professions that they are attracted to include writer, travel agent, tour guide, spiritualist, actor, director, politician, and musician.

Sevens tend to choose professions that allow them to multiply their experiences, either physically or mentally. Their extroverted nature allows them to gel well with people, exert influence on others, and mold their social environment.

Some of the most popular individuals who are Sevens include Leonardo DiCaprio, Robin Williams, Malcolm Forbes, Joe Biden, Wolfgang Mozart, Steven Spielberg, Brad Pitt, Ram Dass, Benjamin Franklin, Bruce Willis, Jim Carrey, Elton John, John F. Kennedy, and Ted Turner.

Personal Growth

Sevens grow by leaps and bounds and witness great growth in their personalities and character when they follow the developmental steps given below:

1. Becoming Aware of Impulses

As a Seven, you should be aware of your innate impulsive nature. You should start observing your impulses whenever they arise instead of giving in to them automatically. This would mean that you may have to let go of a lot of the impulses that arise and become a better judge of the ones that are worth acting upon.

With practice, you will learn to observe when impulses arise, identify which ones to act upon, and focus on them with all your energy without becoming scattered. This will not only make you get in touch with your inner guide but will also make you more comfortable in your skin.

2. Learn to Listen

Listening to other people is an important skill that you need to inculcate. When you listen, you may find that what other people have to say is actually quite interesting which will allow you to learn many new things that can open wide new avenues for you.

Similarly, you need to learn to sit still and appreciate silence and solitude. There is no need to always keep distracting yourself. Constant noise and distraction is a sign that you are trying to protect yourself from the ever-present anxiety. Instead, learn to tone down the external stimulation and trust yourself to live with less. When you concentrate your energy on the things that you choose to do, rather than giving in to impulses, you will find that you are more satisfied with your life.

3. Take your time to form judgments

You should know that you need not have everything, every experience, and every sensation immediately. More often than not, whatever it is that you are looking to acquire will still be available tomorrow. You should give yourself time enough so you can be in a better position to determine whether that thing is good for you.

Taking some time off things will also give you enough mental space to successfully assimilate your experiences and ideas. This can lead to breakthroughs in your life that can reverberate and positively benefit others around you.

4. Choose quality over quantity

When you are choosing your experiences, always go for quality over quantity. The best way to have quality experiences is to give your fullest attention to the experiences you are going through at any given time. If you are always anticipating experiences that are way in the future, you are going to miss out on the present ones which will not only undermine your ability to be satisfied but also makes you anxious and frustrated.

5. Set your goals wisely

Whatever you choose to do, make sure that you think of the long run and how that thing is going to pan out. As the saying goes, careful what you wish for, you just might get it. Similarly, think of the long-term ramifications of the things that you might want. Don't choose to aim for something that you might end up becoming disappointed by, or that might cause you great unhappiness.

Though it is easy for you to learn new things and jump from one to the next, have one major field in which you specialize and keep the rest as appendices, hobbies, or extra-curricular interests that complement your main goal. This will ensure that you have a path laid out for you, which you can journey with your characteristic vigor and excitement.

CHAPTER 16

Enneagram Type 8: The Challenger

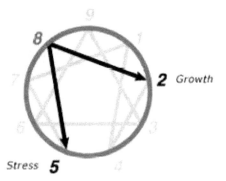

E ights are assertive, strong, and self-
confident. Their natures make them
decisive individuals who are to the
point, protective, and resourceful. However,
they have a tendency to be egotistical and
domineering as well. Eights have a deep urge
to control their environment and other people
to the point that they sometimes get
confrontational and intimidating.

Eights have a problem with their temper
which makes them particularly vulnerable. At
their best, Eights are able to achieve true self-
mastery and use their strength to improve

others' lives, become magnanimous, inspiring, and heroic.

Overview

Eights are termed The Challenger since they enjoy challenging others as well as being challenged, which allows them to exceed themselves in some way. Eights are particularly charismatic individuals that have the psychological and physical abilities to influence others into following them into all kinds of endeavors— be it starting a business, reconstructing a city, waging war, or keeping peace.

Eights are endowed with enormous vitality and willpower and when they exercise these capacities in the world, they feel most alive.

Their abundant energy is spent chiefly in leaving a mark on their environment. However, they also try to keep their environment, and other people, secure ensuring that no harm comes to those they care about. Eights understand, at quite an early age, that they require will power, persistence, strength, and resilience – qualities that they seek to develop early on.

Some common traits of Eights include:

- Eights have the basic desire to protect themselves and be in control of their life and destiny

- Eights have the basic fear of being harmed and controlled by others

- Eights are termed 'The Maverick' with a Seven-Wing, and with a Nine-Wing, 'The Bear'.

- Their key motivations lie in being self-reliant, and to prove their strengths while resisting their weaknesses.

Healthy Eights

In their healthy state, Eights are highly resourceful and have an affirmative attitude that drives them onward. They have a great passion for life that enables them to make things happen. They are natural leaders, honorable and authoritative, who have a commanding presence. They are grounded enough to have the 'common sense' to be decisive about practical problems.

Eights have it in them to face criticism and opposition as they know that their decisions cannot please everyone. However, as much as possible, they try to look after the interests of people under them without playing favorites. Their talents and equanimity are used in the construction of a better world for everyone.

Average Eights

Eights are rugged individuals who prefer to stand alone, more than any other type. They will resist being indebted to people and will refuse to succumb to social conventions. They are able to defy and overcome shame, fear, and concern regarding the consequences of their actions.

Though Eights do fear physical harm, the fear of being controlled and disempowered is much greater in them. Their toughness and the ability to take physical punishment without protest is a double-edged sword as they can take their health for granted and overlook the well-being of those that follow.

Although Eights are extremely industrious, this comes at the price of losing emotional touch with other people in their lives. Many who are close to them may be confounded by their emotional unavailability, which disrupts Eights' emotional life further.

Unhealthy Eights

Unhealthy Eights will do anything in their strength to protect their feelings for they are desperately afraid of being emotionally hurt. Their inner vulnerability is hidden by a layer of emotional armor that gives them their tough façade.

Because of their emotional bluntness, Eights are frequently misunderstood that distances them from people. They are afraid that people will reject them and, in order to defend themselves, they reject others first.

The more they try to protect themselves by building up their egos, the more sensitive they get to any real or imaginary slight to their abilities, their authority, and self-respect. The more they try to make themselves immune to pain, the more they end up 'shutting down' emotionally.

Development Levels

Healthy Development Levels

Level 1

Eights at their best are merciful, self-restrained, forbearing, and magnanimous. They master their selves by surrendering to a higher authority. They are very courageous, and will even put their selves in jeopardy to attain their vision. They are true heroes that end up achieving historical greatness.

Level 2

At this stage, Eights are strong, self-confident, and self-assertive for they have learned to stand up for the things that they need. They have a resourceful attitude and a passion to move forward.

Level 3

Eights at this stage are natural leaders that people look up to. They are not only commanding and authoritative but also decisive that makes things happen. They provide and protect their people, carrying them along with their strength, and as such become the champions of people.

Average Development levels

Level 4

At this stage for Eights, being self-sufficient, financially independent, and have resources enough to pursue their tasks are important considerations. This allows them to pragmatic and enterprising, rugged individuals that they are. They take risks, work hard but end up denying their own emotional requirements.

Level 5

At this stage, Eights try to dominate their environment and other people. They want to know that other people are behind them and are supporting their efforts. Eights at this stage are like those bosses whose word is the law.

They are boastful, expansive, and swaggering. Eights are egocentric, have overbearing pride, and will impose their vision on everyone, not treating others as equal and with respect.

Level 6

At this stage, Eights become intimidating and combating just to get their way. They may even end up becoming belligerent, confrontational, and may divide people between friends and enemies. They see everything as a challenge to them from which they must not back down.

Eights may use threats and retaliations just to make people obey them, and to keep them insecure. However, such treatment makes others resent Eights and they may even group together against them.

Unhealthy Development Levels

Level 7

At this stage, Eights manifest their unhealthy and extreme side. They will defy all attempts by other people to control them. They become dictatorial and ruthless, and many end up becoming outlaws, criminals, and con-artists. To protect their inner vulnerability, they become hard-hearted and out of sync with their emotions, sometimes even immoral and violent.

Level 8

As they regress further, Eights begin to develop delusional ideas of power and invincibility. They may think they are omnipotent and invulnerable, thereby displaying a sort of megalomania. They may extend themselves recklessly without much support.

Level 9

At their worst, Eights become dangerous to others as well as themselves. They will destroy everything that doesn't conform to their ideas and will. They may become murderous, vengeful, and barbaric, especially when they perceive danger. Their tendencies border on sociopathy and antisocial personality disorder.

Symbols

When self-confident Eights move in the direction of stress and disintegration, they become fearful and secretive at Five. On the other hand, controlling and lustful Eights, moving in the direction of growth and integration, become caring, open-hearted, and caring like healthy Twos.

Examples

Eights are true leaders of people, having an inspiring and charismatic character that people can get behind. Their decisive and dominating personalities lend best to careers like activists, politicians, managers, military personnel, athletes, executives, governors, and the like.

Try as they might, they would never succeed in careers in which they are forced to follow someone else's tune. Some of the people who are the best examples of Eights are as follows:

Alec Baldwin, Jack Nicholson, Frank Sinatra, Pablo Picasso, Sean Connery, Russel Crowe, Richard Wagner, Indira Gandhi, Sean Penn, Mikhail Gorbachev, Matt Damon, Courtney Love, Serena Williams, Keith Richards, Ernest Hemingway, and Martin Luther King Jr.

Personal Growth

Eights grow by leaps and bounds and witness positive transformations in their personalities and character when they follow the developmental steps given below:

1. Learn Self-restraint and Forbearance

As Eights, you should learn to act with self-restraint. True power lies not in asserting your will on others when you can but in forbearance and tolerance of other people. Your real strength lies in your ability to uplift and inspire people.

When you are caring, people will not take advantage of you, which will allow you to do more things. As such, you can show your greatness of heart and secure loyalty and devotion of others rather than submitting others under your will.

2. Learn to Yield

Though it can be difficult to do so, learn to yield to others from time to time. More often than not, there's not much at stake and you can allow others to have their way without fearing for the power struggle.

Your desire to dominate other people all the time is a sign that your ego is starting to inflate. This is a dangerous sign that serious conflicts in the future are inevitable.

3. Let people know they are important

As an Eight, it can feel that the world is conspiring against you but nothing can be further from the truth. Remember that most people in your life care about you and look up to you. Even when you are fixated on things and make things tough for them, they stick by you. That affection is something that you should let in from time to time.

Opening yourself up to people won't make you wake. Instead, it will confirm and re-establish the strength and support in your life. Thinking that people are against you will only alienate you and convert your fears into self-fulfilling prophecies. Know the people that are on your side, and let them know that they are important to you.

4. Love People, not Power

Eights tend to value power more than they should. Acquiring power, through position, wealth, or force, gives them the ability to do what they want. But people will not love or follow you because of your power. Know that whatever power you accumulate will come inevitably at a physical and emotional cost. If you want to have people that you love by your side, it cannot be through power and coercion, rather through understanding and respect.

CHAPTER 17

Enneagram Type 9: The Peacemaker

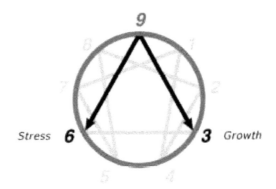

Nines are stable, accepting, and trustworthy individuals. They tend to be optimistic, supportive, and creative and are willing to go along with other people in order to keep the peace. They are averse to conflicts and will do everything to ensure that things go smoothly.

However, they also tend to become complacent as they simplify problems and turn away from anything that is upsetting to them. Their main problems tend to concern stubbornness and inertia. When they are at their best, Nines are all-embracing and indomitable. As such, they are able to bring people together and be the arbiter of peace.

Overview

Nines are termed the Peacemaker as they are devoted, like no other type, to the pursuit of inner and outer peace for others and themselves. They are the spiritualists who yearn for cosmic as well as human connection. Nines work to establish peace of mind within just as they try to establish harmony in the world.

Even though Nines are spiritually oriented in the world, their type is in the Instinctive Center. That means they are well-grounded in their bodies as well as the physical world. It is not exactly a contradiction as only by being in touch with their instincts are they able to generate incredible elemental strength and magnetism.

Some common traits of Nines include:

- Nines have the desire to establish inner stability and 'peace of mind'

- Nines fear loss and separation

- Nines are termed the Referee with an Eight-Wing, and The Dreamer with a One-Wing.

- Nines are mainly motivated by the need to create harmony in their environment, avoiding conflicts, preserving things, and resisting things that may disturb or upset them.

Healthy Nines

Healthy Nines are in balance with their center and are akin to a river that carries everyone along effortlessly. They are peace lovers and will always look for the best way to reach a peaceful resolution to conflicts. Being the mediators and peacemakers that they are, they have a unique gift of understanding and sympathizing with mutually exclusive viewpoints and find a middle path.

Nines are also sometimes seen as the Enneagram crown since its symbol is at the top and includes the whole. As such, they have the strengths of all other types as well. At their best, Nines are able to embrace everyone and have an unconquerable spirit. They are not only attuned to the spiritual world but are also grounded in reality which makes them leaders in spiritual thought and religions.

Average Nines

When Nines are cut off from their instinctual center, they end up becoming detached and remote. To compensate for the loss of their instinctual center, Nines withdraw into their minds and their fantasies. The imbalance of their instinctive energies can lead to psychic inactivity and inertness.

These instinctive energies, when not used, end up damming up the source that feeds it. Without an internal anchor, Nines tend to get swayed by other people, melt into them, or follow their own static and purposeless daydreams. Thought they have the qualities of all other types, the only type that they are not like is the Nine itself.

Unhealthy Nines

Nines are averse to disturbing aspects of life and will look to seek out peace and comfort. They respond to the suffering and pain of life by resorting to a peacefulness that is not attained from within but is premature. As such, they live in either denial or a state of false spirituality.

Nines look to run away from the contradictions and tensions of life by trying to get transcend them. They may even try to simplify the problems and look for painless and simple solutions to the problems. Nines tend to focus on the silver linings as a way of ensuring that their peace of mind remains undisturbed.

However, Nines must not deny that darker aspects of life, for only when the two perspectives are brought together, they are able to rise above them. Nines must also realize that the best way is to go through life, not to escape into so-called Buddhahood prematurely.

Development Levels

Healthy Development Levels

Level 1

At their best, Nines are autonomous and deeply fulfilled. They are steady under stress and content in their lives, mainly because they are aware and present in whatever it is they are doing. They are one with themselves and are also able to form profound relationships with other people.

Level 2

Nines at this stage are serene, emotionally stable, receptive of other people, and unselfconscious. They are trusting of their own selves as well as of others. They are generally at ease with life and live innocently and simply. They are patient with people, good-natured, unpretentious, and truly pleasant people.

Level 3

At this stage, Nines are supportive, reassuring, and optimistic individuals. They have a healing and calming influence that fosters harmony and brings people together. They can synthesize different viewpoints together, communicate well with people, and mediate between parties.

Average Development levels

Level 4

For Nines, fear is the main source of conflict. That is why they will go to great lengths to be accommodating, say 'yes' to things that may not ring right to them, and even become self-effacing. At this stage, Nines end up falling into conventional expectations and roles and use stock philosophies and ready-made answers to deflect others.

Level 5

Though Nines may be active, they remain inattentive, unreflective, and disengaged. Because they do not want to be affected by others, they become complacent and unresponsive. They may walk away from issues or ignore them.

Their thinking, as such, becomes ruminative and hazy, and they find comfort in fantasies, tuning out of reality, and becoming oblivious to things around them. Their indifference becomes palpable as they become emotionally inert and shy away from exerting themselves or focusing on problems.

Level 6

At this stage, Nines try to appease others and will look to have peace at any cost. They look to simplify and minimize problems. When confronted with hard problems, Nines become resigned and fatalistic, as though they think that nothing could be done to usher in change.

Nines may resort to wishful thinking and their indolence can end up frustrating and infuriating other people.

Unhealthy Development Levels

Level 7

At this stage, Nines are undeveloped and repressed individuals. They feel that they are incapable of facing their problems, which makes them obstinate. They look to disassociate themselves from all sorts of

conflicts and their neglect can be dangerous
to themselves as well as others.

Level 8

At this stage, Nines disassociate from their
surroundings so much that they become
numb and unable to function. They look to
block out even the awareness of things that
could potentially be problematic to them.

Level 9

At their worst, Nines become catatonic and
severely disoriented. They abandon
themselves and turn inwards into their shells.
Their mental state deteriorates to schizoid
personality disorders and there is even the
danger of the development of multiple
personalities.

Symbols

When Nines move in the direction of stress
and disintegration, they become worried and
anxious at Six. On the other hand, when
slothful and procrastinating Nines move in
the direction of growth and integration, they
become energetic, and highly developed like
Three.

Examples

Being Peacemakers and Mediators, Nines are able to excel in numerous careers. They are ideally suited as healers, doctors, yoga and meditation instructors, social workers, religious workers, caretakers, and counselors.

Some of the people who exemplify Nines are as follows:

Morgan Freeman, George Lucas, Toby McGuire, Walt Disney, Joseph Campbell, Carl Jung, George W. Bush, Jeff Bridges, Woody Harrelson, Carl Rogers, Abraham Lincoln, and Jack Johnson.

Personal Growth

Nines can grow tremendously in character and ability when they follow the developmental steps given below:

Be Independent

As a Nine, you should examine your tendency to get along with people and how much you go out of your way to keep the peace. Know that you cannot always give in to the wishes of others and still feel satisfied. That is why you should stand your ground and always be yourself. Being independent is the only way you are able to truly be there for other people when they need you.

Pay Attention

As a Nine, you have to learn to give attention to things that are going on around you. More than that, you have to exert yourself out of your lethargy and indolence. The more you are able to focus your attention and become an active participant in your surroundings, the more grounded you will be. It will also keep you mentally and emotionally engaged.

Become aware of your Shadow

Learn to give due consideration to the darker aspects within you, such as anxieties, aggression, and other negative feelings. They are a part of you and affect you physically and emotionally whether you acknowledge it or not.

These negative emotions automatically find their way out that disrupts peace and harmony in your life. It is better to get them out and clear the air, or at least become aware that they exist within you.

Examine your part

Whatever problems you may find yourself in always examine how your actions or inactions have contributed to them. This is much easier said than done but is nevertheless something that must be endeavored.

You must realize the role you have played in the conflicts that have arisen. To do this, you must be ready to sacrifice your peace of mind so that you can have the satisfaction of true relationships in the future.

As a Nine, you should have a regular exercise routine as it will help you become aware of your body. Exercising regularly doesn't just improve your health, but also build up your self-discipline. As you develop your body awareness, you will find it easier to focus and concentrate your attention in all areas of your life too. It also enables you to give a channel to the aggressive side inside of you. This will ensure that you get in touch with the darker aspects of yourself and keep them from disrupting your life.

CONCLUSION

The Enneagram as a system of personality categorization works so well to illuminate one's inner being as it forces us to confront our weaknesses as well as your strengths. Insofar as we are able to focus on the things that help us grow, and realize the tendencies that lead us astray, we will be able to give expression to ourselves in full.

As it is a source of great information that is at once individual and supra-personal, it brings us to realize that path that leads to salvation as espoused by Christ. Though the Enneagram is fraught with religious themes and lessons, its psychological as well as scientific underpinnings cannot be foregone.

When an individual comes to terms with his/her shortcomings, understands the actions that must be taken, then the path towards growth becomes palpable. The path of disintegration is paved with fear and insecurities, but the one that leads to growth and the achievement of one's full potential can only be undertaken with love, for oneself as well as others.

The Enneagram makes us understand our true potential, and once we realize the divine within, we are able to rise above the trifles that bog us down and create a life that is grounded on love and compassion.

The soul that resides within us takes us multiple forms – as described by the Nine types – and each brings about its own special abilities and capacities. None of the types are necessarily superior or inferior to any other and are equally invaluable in the world. Their different combinations bring about the plethora of individualities in their different development levels – all seeking, consciously or unconsciously, to be better than they are.

Life is a chaotic place where, over time, humans have come to understand the mode of being that can lead them to a higher level of consciousness. Though different religions and systems espouse different paths, all true paths ultimately converge into one. That is where one is able to find the anointed one – Christ – and know him to be the symbol of the hero that emerges from the deep darkness to rise like the sun.

Regardless of where one comes from, the human capacity for good and evil is the same and only through awareness, love, and understanding one is able to learn to tame the devil, and give expression to the divine within. That is the only way forward to peace, harmony, and most of all, oneness.